Black Berry,
Sweet Juice

Lawrence Hill

Black Berry, Sweet Juice

On Being Black and White in Canada

Harper*Flamingo*Canada

www.harpercanada.com

HarperCollins books may be purchased for
educational, business, or sales promotional use.
For information please write:
Special Markets Department,
HarperCollins Canada,
55 Avenue Road, Suite 2900,
Toronto, Ontario, Canada M5R 3L2

First edition

Canadian Cataloguing in Publication Data

Hill, Lawrence, 1957–
Black berry, sweet juice : on being black and white
in Canada

ISBN 0-00-200020-2

1. Hill, Lawrence, 1957–
2. Racially mixed people – Canada – Biography.
3. Interracial marriage – Canada.
4. Black Canadians – Race identity.
5. Canada – Race relations.
6. Authors, Canadian (English) – 20th century –
   Biography.
I. Title.

PS8565.I444Z53 2001   305.8'044'0092
C2001-901185-7
PR9199.3.H45Z47 2001

HC 9 8 7 6 5 4 3 2 1

Printed and bound in the United States
Set in Stempel Garamond

For my beloved daughter,
Caroline May Savoie Hill,
who is black, white,
and everything in between

The blacker the berry
The sweeter the juice
                    —*a saying among North American blacks*

The blacker the berry
The sweeter the juice
But if you get too black
It ain't no use
                    —*the saying as re-engineered by others*
                    and passed along to me by my father,
                    Daniel G. Hill III

Contents

Part Three   **Sticks and Stones**

Introduction

It is common to the point of being a cliché for a black person to want to connect with other black people. I learned this in my earliest childhood. Whenever my father walked through a supermarket in the Toronto suburb of Don Mills, with or without my white mother, he would smile or nod his head or stop to chew the fat if he bumped into someone, even a complete stranger, who was black. When we were driving in the car, he would erupt from time to time with "Hey, kids, look, there's a black bus driver!" This came, of course, from his leaving the largely black city of Washington, D.C., and moving in the early 1950s to Toronto, where, as Dad has said, you could walk all day and not see a black person. He taught me the importance of connecting with other black people, especially when there were so few of us around.

I did see some black people from time to time when I was growing up: at family gatherings in the States, or when our relatives came up to Toronto to visit the Canadian Hills, as they called us; when we visited special family friends once or twice a year; here and there on the street, by accident. I came to look forward to those occasional intersections with

1

black folks. I felt some confidence that if I approached a black person with an open, smiling face, I'd end up in an interesting, friendly conversation. Indeed, I once carried that trusting sense of affinity to an absurd extreme when I was travelling in Utrecht, a city in the Netherlands. It was 1974, I was seventeen, I had a Canadian flag stitched onto my knapsack, and I somehow managed to get myself completely lost downtown, without any idea how to find my way back to the youth hostel where I was staying. What was I to do, without a word of Dutch?

I stood on a street corner for a few minutes, contemplating my fate, when suddenly, across the street, I noticed a tall black man who looked to be in his mid-twenties. I walked right over to him and asked, straight up, "Hey, man, I'm totally lost, could you tell me . . . ?" He put his hand up, smiled and began telling me, in French, that he did not speak English. It turned out that he was a foreign student from Zaire. Although I switched over to French and got the directions I needed, I felt colossally idiotic for having assumed that because this man was black, he would speak English. He seemed quite indulgent and was perhaps touched to see a young North American black kicking around Holland on his own. We repaired to the closest bar, where he bought me a beer. It turned out that we did have much to yak about—what life was like for African students in Europe at the time, and what it was like for blacks in Canada.

From my earliest years, then, I was seeking out links with black folks here and there, wherever I could find them. But several decades would pass before I began—with the research for this book—to make a concerted effort to meet people who, like me, were of mixed race. People with one black and one white parent. It was unusual for me to see black people in the 1960s in Don Mills—outside the walls of my own house, at least—and I never saw people of mixed race. I discovered, very early, that some people had strange ideas about the children of interracial unions, and seemed inclined to believe that life for us would be miserable. Indeed, when I was twelve, my best friend was a white girl who looked sixteen. We must have been a funny-looking set of friends because when I was twelve, I looked about eight. In any case, Marilyn (as I shall name her) and I formed a fast friendship, and she bonded immediately with my father— perhaps because she had no relationship whatsoever with her own. Marilyn's mother would embarrass the dickens out of me by singing my praises to her own children. "Look how well Larry does in school. Why can't you be like that, Marilyn?" These comments, which made me squirm and wish I could vanish from their home, at the same time elicited my profound sympathy for Marilyn. But astoundingly, this same mother who thought I was doing so well once took me aside and said, "Frankly, Larry, don't you think it is terrible, mixing races like that? It ruins the children! How are they to make their way in life?" It helped that I had a touch of arrogance as a twelve-year-old and thought this woman ignorant. Much better to believe that she was ill-informed than to feel hurt by her comments. I told her that she was imagining problems that weren't there.

Connecting with black people in a land with few clustered black communities has been a lifelong journey for me. Connecting with people with one black and one white parent, as I did while researching this book, was a completely new experience. We had a great deal to say to each other. And I found a great deal to write about.

One of the first things I discovered is that my own experience of race, including my concept of my own racial identity, is shaded quite differently from that of my parents. They were both born and raised in the United States, and their racial identities were clearly delineated all their lives. The America of their youth and early adulthood was replete with laws that banned interracial marriages and upheld segregation in every domain of public life. One of the most personally telling details came to me from my mother, who was working as a secretary for a Democratic senator when she met my father in Washington, D.C., in 1953: "When I started dating your father, even the federal government cafeterias were segregated." In the United States, there was never any doubt that my father was first and foremost a black man. Or that my mother was a white woman. And there is no question that, had my siblings and I been raised in the United States, we would have been identified—in school, on the street, in community centres, among friends—as black.

But my parents threw their unborn children a curve ball. They came to Toronto right after they married, had us, and we all stayed here. They had had enough of racial divisions in their country of birth. And although they spent their lives at the forefront of the Canadian human rights movement, they were also happy and relieved to set up in suburban, white, middle-class Toronto, where race faded (most of the time) into the background.

When I was growing up, I didn't spend much time thinking about who I was or where I fit in. I was too busy tying my shoelaces, brushing my teeth, learning to spell, swinging baseball bats, and shooting hockey pucks. But once in a while, just as my guard was down, questions of my own identity would leap like a cougar from the woods and take a bite out of my backside.

I have always been fascinated by personal identity—how it is shaped and transformed. Your identity, to a large degree, reflects the society you live in. I imagine myself stranded on a lush tropical island. Until the search party finds me, all I have to do is survive. I'm going to build a shelter, eat mangoes, crack coconuts, snare quail and net fish. During this extended time out, I'm not going to be thinking very much about the colour of my skin (unless it is getting sunburnt) or my racial identity. These thoughts won't preoccupy me unless tourists invade my paradise and start looking at me, and I start looking at them, and we begin the endless dance of adjusting how we see others, how we want to be seen, and how we see ourselves.

Race becomes an issue as a result of environmental factors. The average white kid growing up in a totally white suburb doesn't have to think of himself or herself as white. For a huge portion of my childhood, I was very much like that white kid. But gradually, as imperceptibly as the movement of the hour hand around the clock, my environment started talking to me and making me aware that I was different, that I could never truly be white. There's nothing like being called "nigger" to let you know that you're not white. It didn't happen often. But it happened enough to awaken me.

Learning that I wasn't white, however, wasn't the same as learning that I was black. Indeed, for the longest time I didn't learn what I was—only what I wasn't. In the strange and unique society that was Canada, I was allowed to grow up in a sort of racial limbo. People knew what I wasn't—white or black—but they sure couldn't say what I was.

I have black American cousins, of both lighter and darker complexions, who attended segregated schools and grew up in entirely black communities. They had no reason to doubt

5

their racial identity. That identity was wrapped around them, like a snug towel, at the very moment of birth. In 1977, when I decided to take a year off university, I went to visit my cousins in Brooklyn before flying to Europe. That planned excursion, in itself, must have appeared to them a quintessentially white thing to do. But they were gracious and welcoming, and they took me into their home, to the jazz bars, the basketball courts, the Empire State Building, even to Broadway to see a play by Bertolt Brecht. My cousin Richard Flateau—who was a few years younger than I was and still in high school—took me under his wing, and was remarkably patient until I asked if he liked to play squash. Before he could think to censor himself, an indignant retort exploded from his lips: "Larry! That's a *white* folks' game!"

The truth of the matter was that I loved squash. It was fast, and intense, and let me smash out all of my aggressions on a pliant rubber ball. It was one of my favourite sports, right up there with long-distance running (another activity that wasn't exactly a magnet for black kids at the time). I got so hooked on squash that, as a teenager, I would borrow my parents' car and pick up a friend and drive ten kilometres to the grounds of the private, completely white Upper Canada College. It had lovely squash courts, and on summer evenings nobody checked to see whether you belonged there.

Today, looking back, I find irony in that image. There I was, son of a black American Second World War veteran and a white American civil rights activist, playing squash in Canada at a private school where tuition fees exceeded the annual income of—well, certainly of many poor black Americans.

These days, I have been thinking about that seventeen-year-old mixed-race squash player growing up in Toronto's middle-class suburbs, surrounded almost entirely by white people. I think of the many factors that contributed to my sense of identity, and of how fluid and malleable that sense of identity was and, to a certain degree, still is. There were days when I went straight from my exclusive, private boys' high school to family events populated by black relatives or friends who idolized the icons and heroes of my child-hood—Angela Davis, with her intelligence and her kick-ass afro; sprinters Tommy Smith and John Carlos, with their black-gloved fists raised on the Olympic podium in Mexico City; Muhammad Ali, who stood up to the white man and spoke the words that moved the world: "I ain't got no quarrel with the Viet Cong."

I bounced back and forth between studying Latin, play-ing squash, and revering black American cultural icons, but who exactly was I? How do you navigate the waters of identity with one black and one white parent? How have other Canadians who share the same mixed-race back-ground managed it? What does it mean to be black and white in Canada?

These are the questions that I set out to examine in this book.

• • •

This is my personal account of identity, and any biases, lim-itations, or inaccuracies—and there surely will be some—are mine alone. Nevertheless, I wanted *Black Berry, Sweet Juice* to reach beyond my own world, and to include the voices and observations of other people who had one black and one white parent. The process of finding those voices has changed my life, and has had a profound effect on the way I have come to understand identity.

At first, my idea was to take informal notes, chat with a few people, and use their insights to broaden the scope of my own writing. But as the interviews began, something amazing happened: people took me into their confidence, responded to the most intimate and impertinent of questions, and opened up astounding worlds to me. I felt an immediate and visceral connection with almost all of the men and women I interviewed.

I did not interview children, with the exception of my nephew David Hill, of Toronto, who was eleven at the time. David informed me that he was "part black" and that anybody who had a problem with that "would eventually find out the truth." He also mentioned the racism in our own family history—he was referring to a few white relatives who had cut off my mother when she married a black man—and calmly asserted, perhaps for the benefit of those who abandoned my mother, that "the world started out with black people—white people and everybody else evolved from black people."

The interviews began to blossom, and eventually took me to people from Vancouver, Edmonton, Calgary, Saskatoon, Hamilton, Burlington, Oakville, Georgetown, Mississauga, Toronto, Montreal, Halifax, and Sydney. In all, I interviewed thirty-four Canadians who each had one black and one white parent. The mixed-race interview subjects ranged in age from eighteen to sixty-one. I also interviewed nine other people—seven black and two white—who had experiences and insights that I wanted to learn more about. The interviews included sessions with my father, mother, brother, and sister. Most of the people I met agreed to be interviewed on the record, but two women—"Sara" in London, Ontario, and "Amanda" in Saskatoon, Saskatchewan—will remain anonymous.

My interviews were personal and literary adventures. I found people solely by word of mouth. I am not an academic, and this was not a scholarly process. I do acknowledge, however, that the observations in *Black Berry, Sweet Juice* may be limited by the fact that I found only two interview subjects over the age of fifty, and only one person (to my knowledge) who was homosexual. I suspect that I would have heard a broader range of comments if I had been able to find more people who were well into and beyond midlife. Without doubt, there is also much to be learned from how gays and lesbians of mixed race relate to each other and deal with questions of racial and sexual identity, but somebody else will have to write those books.

. . .

Lately, I have been looking at some family photos and mulling over what they mean to me. In my home office, I have some thirty framed shots of relatives. There are my three children, running, cavorting, picking apples. The eldest, Geneviève, is eleven, and I wonder how she will come to see herself, racially, as she moves into adolescence and adulthood. She has been a passionate ballerina for six years, and you don't find a world much whiter than that, not even in Oakville, where we live. She knows who she is and where she comes from, and has had much contact with the black side of her family—but the girl has blue eyes and skin even lighter than mine, and I can see that if she is going to assert her own blackness one day, she may have to work hard at it. Nine-year-old Caroline, the middle child, is the darkest of my three, and has that uncanny middle-child ability to relate to anybody of any age. I have noticed that she already bonds particularly vigorously with black women. Andrew, who is seven, is for the time being about as interested in race as he would be in nuclear physics. Interestingly, though, he has already called out a few times, "I'm not black, I'm white," and shot a look my way to test for a reaction. He looks white, too. I have a refined radar system for identifying folks of mixed race, but in a crowd, I'm not sure I could pick out Andrew.

Would you like to know how my children would once have been categorized, racially? Quadroons. They have a father who is supposedly half black and a mother who is white, and that parentage, according to the traditional racial definition blender, would have made them quadroons. Quadroons, of course, were most definitely black, and enslaved like the rest of us in Canada and the United States. Quadroon women were favoured by slave owners for features deemed exotic and sexy but not too black, thank you very much. I shudder to imagine children who looked just like mine dancing in the infamous Quadroon Balls in New Orleans, where hot-looking young women were bought and consumed until they were no longer young or beautiful.

My children stand on the shoulders of a world that has demonized, enslaved, and raped countless people exactly like them. Today in Canada, in 2001, black people still contend with racism at every level of society. And yet, the way my children will define themselves, and be defined by others, remains up for grabs. They look white. But if you take a second look, if you have any kind of eye for this at all, they also look black. On the one hand, how they look has everything to do with their sense of themselves. You can be sure that if they looked obviously black, they would be treated as black, regardless of their family make-up. On the other hand, their appearance has nothing—and should have nothing—to do with who they are. Racial identity is about how you see yourself, about how you construct a sense of belonging, community, awareness, and allegiance. You can be as dark as the night or as light as my son, Andrew, but if you feel you belong and you show it, you are black.

But is that all? Can you be other things, too? Am I just black? Am I not also a man? a son? a father? a runner? a writer? a heterosexual? a Canadian? a lover of the outdoors? If I am all of these things, just as any person reading this page is the sum total of a lifetime of experiences and interactions, can I not also be white? Can I be black and white, all in the same breath?

Let me forget, for a moment, all the notions that I have been told about race since I was old enough to understand the word. And let me imagine, for a moment, that I can choose for myself how I see myself. To this date, I have for the most part seen myself as black. With the exception of my mother, there are no white relatives in the photographs on the walls of my home office. Photos of my father, paternal grandparents, and paternal great-grandparents have all been framed carefully, along with pictures of my children. Why no white relatives? One reason is that my black American relatives, who lived in Brooklyn, Washington, D.C., Baltimore, and North Carolina, were much closer to us and much easier to visit than my mother's family. Apart from her twin, Dottie, whom we all adore, we never really got to know my mother's relatives. They lived much farther away, mostly in Arizona and California. Some we rarely visited, others we never met. There was more to it than that, however. My mother spoke negatively of her brothers when we were young, often describing how they gave her a hard time—one of them even questioned her sanity—when she announced that she would be marrying a black man. As a result, as a child I came to nourish a minor grudge against some of these relatives. On my father's side,

11

however, family was like an extension of my own body and psyche.

Nevertheless, I think the sands of identity are shifting once again in my own heart. My mother is aging, and life has been excruciatingly difficult for her in recent years as she has been caring for my father, who is dying of diabetes-related complications. I think Mom wants to right the very real imbalance in family allegiances. At the very least, she wants us to appreciate her family and her family history, and to know who our ancestors were. Recently, she got hold of an old album of photographs, and asked me to look at it with her. I agreed, so as not to hurt her feelings, but once the book opened, my interest went from passive to passionate. I saw some astounding photographs. Two of them, taken in the early 1900s, were of my mom's grand-fathers. One of them, her mother's father, was William Andrew Duryee. My son is named Andrew, and I hadn't even known that he shared the name with my great-grandfather. This man was a wheat and cattle farmer in Webster, South Dakota. Brutal winters, scorching sum-mers—basically, an American version of southern Mani-toba. He was rugged and lean and gaunt and severe, and it looked as if the only rest he knew was when he slept. This was my great-grandfather. A farmer! I started wondering about him. Was he hot-headed and opinionated like my mother? Could he decorticate any topic that landed on his kitchen table, and walk you up one side of his argument and down the other? Was he a Republican? What contact did he have with black people? Poor people? Hell, he looked poor enough in that photo! I wanted to know more about him and his life.

As I probed with questions, I saw a look of contentment in my mother's eyes. We sat together for an hour, flipping through this old album, until my father finally called for her and she got up to help him.

I am going to find out more about William Andrew Duryee. And when I know more about him, I'm going to get a copy of that incredible photograph of the dusty, work-drunk South Dakota farmer, frame it, and find a good place for it in my office. In the meantime, I've got a story to tell you. Part of it is memoir, an examination of my own life through the prism of mixed race. Part of it includes comments and observations from the many people I interviewed of black and white ancestry. Part of it looks at broader social issues dealing in one way or another with mixed race. I hope that how I have come to see not only myself but the world in which I live will enrich the ways that people understand identity, and the ways that we speak to each other.

Part One

Family Matters

You Are

My children once joined me in a meeting with members of a black women's book club, who had asked me to speak with them about my last novel. While I answered questions, the children did their best to put a dent in the prodigious quantity of food laid out for our enjoyment. I always have the hardest time getting Caroline, my middle child, to touch meat of any kind, but that night she dug into jerk chicken as if preparing for famine. This child of mine, who at home would eat plain pasta for days on end if she had her druthers, also tucked into fried plantain, peas and rice, and all sorts of dishes she had never seen before.

A few hours later, we headed out into the muggy Toronto night. Caroline, who was eight at the time, nudged me on the sidewalk, took my hand, and asked, "Daddy, how come black women always cook such good food?"

I stopped walking and looked at her, dumbfounded. I mumbled something about the fact that her own white mother was a good cook. She shot right back at me, "Yes, but every time we meet black women, there is always so much food around, and it is always so good. It's not like that, not all the time, when we go into white people's houses."

We resumed walking, and I swung her hand as we approached the car. Andrew, my son, was busy kicking a tennis ball, but Geneviève was paying close attention and chose to back up her little sister: "Actually, Daddy, it's true what she is saying."

This conversation was beginning to remind me of all the times I had heard my own father dismantle generalizations about black people when I was a child. His own words seemed to tumble from my mouth as I took on my two daughters.

"Look, Caroline. And you, too, Geneviève. Yes, we've had some fine meals in the homes of some black women. But not all black women can cook. I know one or two who can barely boil an egg."

My daughters howled in laughter at that image. Watching them cramped over on the sidewalk, I smiled and thought, Ain't that somethin'? Something about these kids really looks black. When they settled down, I continued.

"We've been to the homes of a few black women, and it so happens that you got some great stuff to eat. But you've had some amazing meals in the homes of white women, too. What about *Tante* Jacqueline in Quebec? What about Silvana DiGiacomo in Italy? What about your mom? Wouldn't you say she is a good cook? But every time you have a good meal at a white person's home, you don't walk out of the door later and say to yourself, 'Boy, can white people ever cook!' "

They nodded thoughtfully. But several months later, when we stepped into a Christmas potluck feast set up by some black writers in Toronto, Caroline nudged me again: "Daddy! What was I telling you before?"

My children don't get a great deal of contact with black culture. They see my father and siblings from time to time.

Sometimes they meet my black friends. Once a year or so, they see my American relatives. I have taken them down to South Carolina and shown them some black history sites. I take them whenever I can to literary or cultural events involving black people. They know that my parents were pioneers in Canada's human rights movement, and they clutched my father's hand proudly when he received the Order of Canada. As a result of these and other points of contact, they are beginning to develop an awareness of black people, and their own sense of how they fit into the overall picture.

Geneviève has a phenomenal ear for music. Every time my brother Dan's voice comes over the radio, she identifies him within the first few seconds. She hits every note when she sings along to pop songs and grudgingly admires jazz vocalists of yesteryear, such as Ella Fitzgerald and Joe Williams. One day, about four years ago, we were driving along the highway and she started listening intently to a male R & B artist on the radio.

"Daddy, what's his name?"

"Luther Vandross."

"He's black, isn't he?"

"Yes. How'd you know?"

"Oh, I don't know. I can just tell."

Over the next months, Geneviève continued the game whenever we were driving. I was astounded at how accurately she guessed the black artists.

"Who's that?"

"Aretha Franklin."

"Black, I bet."

"Yup."

"And this singer, Daddy. I don't know his name. But I can tell you right now he's black."

"Uh-huh. That's Stevie Wonder."

She giggled at that name. Next thing I knew, she was nailing Gladys Knight, Smokey Robinson, James Ingram, Diana Ross, and all sorts of other old black crooners whose stuff was still being played on the easy-listening stations. One day, however, Geneviève got it wrong.

"Who's that?" she said.

"It's Van Morrison." He was singing "Sometimes I Feel Like a Motherless Child."

"He's black, right?"

"Nope."

"Yes, he is!"

"No, honey. He sounds black because he's borrowing from black musical traditions, but he isn't black. He's white. And he's an incredible singer."

"I'll say."

I wonder what understanding my children will have of black people, the black experience, and black culture as they grow older. And I wonder how they will fit into the picture. I wonder especially how Geneviève will manage in her passion, ballet, where one rarely sees black dancers. But they are launched, and all I can do is keep loving them, sharing with them, and bringing good experiences and good people into their lives.

In the fall of 2000, I spoke at a York University conference about mixed-race children. One other speaker presented a wish list of things parents should do to ensure that their mixed-race children develop a healthy sense of identity. I thought the prescription was well intentioned, but absurd. *Just kill me now*, I muttered to myself, *if we all get stuck with the same marching orders.* I reacted by saying it seemed to me that the most important task was to love your children and help them achieve a sense of self-worth. Sure, I acknowledged, fostering racial awareness was good to do . . .

but I didn't want someone to tell me how to do it in between serving breakfast, getting everybody dressed and off to school, overseeing homework, driving kids to lessons, throwing baseballs, playing tag, making dinner, running baths, and reading bedtime stories. The conference made me wonder, however, if I could be doing a better job. And this wondering has led me to reconsider my own childhood experiences, and to think about some of the stories other people told me as I researched this book.

. . .

My childhood was punctuated with sayings about black people. My father's relatives sometimes said, "The blacker the berry, the sweeter the juice." On one level, the meaning is obvious: a raspberry or strawberry that is full and dark and pregnant with its own ripeness is sweeter than its pink, prematurely plucked counterpart. But there is also a sexual undertone to the saying, a suggestion of the myth of the overcharged, overheated, high-performing black body. Presumably, the blacker berry tastes richer, more full, and is juicier. It is waiting to explode in the mouth.

The trouble with this colourful expression is that it has always struck me as a limp-wristed effort to help black people believe that it was okay to be black. It seemed to me sad and pathetic that we even felt a need to pass around a saying like that. But I wasn't the only one who found that the words itched more than they tickled. My father bombed the pious saying to smithereens with his own sarcastic version:

The blacker the berry
The sweeter the juice
But if you get too black
It ain't no use.

I absolutely loved that variation. It pleased me immensely. Why? Because it turned self-affirmation on its head with a mere ten additional words, offering a bittersweet reminder of the hopelessness of being black in a society that doesn't love—or even like—black people.

There were many other sayings. Here is one I remember:

If you're white
You're all right.
If you're brown
Stick around.
If you're black
Stay back.

Black people said these words and laughed. All the sayings underscored the utter futility of being black. In a way, they were sharply political and served to remind us of the facts of life, insofar as black people were concerned. Sometimes, however, the black folks of my childhood and youth went beyond caustic observations of reality and indulged in their own racial stereotypes. These made me uncomfortable, in the same way that racist jokes generally leave me squirming and obliged to protest. My father, for example, complained often and bitterly about CPT—coloured people's time—which he perceived to be a chronic propensity for lateness among black people. Some sort of defective chromosome. You knew, he said, that when blacks organized a community dinner, they'd get the rubber chicken onto your plate at about the time when most civilized folks were climbing into bed. This comment was meant to be funny, when said with the right timing and a dramatic rolling of the eyes. But there was just one problem. For some years, as a child, I actually believed it was true. I was convinced that if black people were called upon to organize something, it would surely go awry.

This kind of humorous stereotyping wasn't unusual for my father. From my earliest years, he gave out mixed signals about black people—signals that complicated my sense of racial identity and racial pride. On the one hand, I sensed his subtle disinclination to involve himself socially with black people, and I experienced his derision whenever black people organized events poorly or got fired from their jobs. Indeed, when he was the director and then the first chair of the Ontario Human Rights Commission, he would sometimes proudly tell us that he was one of the only blacks he knew who had climbed the job ladder and not been humbled by some stupid move such as padding expense accounts or harassing secretaries.

On the other hand, my father spoke with great passion and empathy about human rights and his work in that field. He told spellbinding stories about the history of blacks in Canada. He urged us to watch television documentaries about slavery in Canada and in the United States, expressed delight when we picked up books by black authors, and subscribed to *Ebony*—one of the few black magazines available at the time. I thought *Ebony* was superficial in the extreme, and a silly attempt by black people to imitate the very worst of white people's puff journalism. I find it interesting that I had already, at that young age, internalized the value that it wasn't good enough for black people to do something ordinary, predictable, or shallow. I wanted them to either kick ass or keep quiet and get out of the way. Around the age of ten or twelve, when my father had been speaking to us about atrocities such as the Atlantic slave trade and the Holocaust, I asked him at what point in life I would begin to be responsible for all that was wrong with the world. He answered, "As soon as you are able to do something about the world, you become responsible for its condition." Heavy stuff, indeed.

. . .

My earliest awareness of race, and my first sense of blackness, seemed to spring from warm places. Our house boomed with jazz and blues music on the weekends. Dan, Karen, and I watched countless times—entranced, intrigued—as our parents danced in the living room to the sounds of Joe Williams, Ella Fitzgerald, Count Basie, Billie Holiday, and Duke Ellington. Dad has an amazing voice. When he sang, he waltzed up and down the tunes with a playfulness and irreverence that we found absolutely infectious.

I remember being laid up with the flu when I was four or five. I didn't want to be isolated in my bedroom, so I stretched out on the living room couch. My mother covered me with a blanket, and my father came to me with a glass of apple juice and a question: "Any musical requests, sir?" And I said, "Could you put on Joe Williams?" "Every Day I Have the Blues" began to jump off the record player. I listened to my dad and Williams nailing the notes as Count Basie hammered the piano, and trumpets, trombones, and saxophones erupted with glee. It's one of the most grooving, happiest songs I've ever heard—even if it is about singing the blues.

Nobody loves me
nobody seems to care
between bad luck and trouble
well you know I've had my share.

Just about any words could have flown from Joe Williams's lips and soared, ecstatically, as if to prove that nothing could keep this man from living and loving. Jazz and blues were already showing me the sweet alchemy of trouble and joy that defined black musical expression, and black people themselves.

My brother says that when he was growing up, one of the first artists to stir his sense of racial identity was Billie Holiday. "There was something in her voice that I found very disturbing, a kind of reed-like, mournful soul that made her voice so great. It cut too deep for me, and I found it almost impossible to listen to her because, in a sense, I could really feel the pain of her black experience."

When I asked Dan if he could recall when he first became aware of his race, he pointed back to his early childhood. "We were all in the car with Mom and Dad. I was about five or six. Mom and Dad were talking to us about all the great things that black people had accomplished, and I remember saying I wished I were black, or negro, whatever the word was at the time, and they said, 'You are,' and I felt this absolute sense of pride and wonder. That was the first time it dawned on me that I was black, or part black."

My sister Karen's sense of blackness was also very much developed by the music of our childhood. In her mid-twenties, Karen was living the bohemian, expatriate life in Berlin. She heated her flat with coal, had no elevator to get her up the four long flights to her place, and for years had to share a common toilet with other neighbours, but the one luxury my sister never did without was the family music. On each of my three visits to spend time with her in Berlin, I found tapes and LPs by the jazz and blues singers of our childhood.

There were sharper and more negative moments, however, that told us in no uncertain terms that being black wasn't necessarily good.

I experienced the odd incident as a child, such as being called a nigger at the hockey rink or at school. I used to play pick-up games of lacrosse at the local recreation centre, and I remember worrying, as I headed over there, whether the others would let me play. One time, as I walked a bicycle with a flat tire, two older boys approached me and spat in my face as they went by. I was shocked, but kept walking as I wiped the warm, nauseating saliva from my face. For a long time, I wondered why they had done that. Was it because they saw me as black, or at least as different from them? The incident shamed me, and I didn't tell anyone about it.

I don't recall early moments with family members that gave me a negative sense of race, but my siblings do. Karen, as a child, visited our maternal grandfather in Arizona. While there, she was reproached for sunbathing too much. Karen has the darkest complexion of the three of us and is certainly the fastest to tan, and my grandfather let her know that he did not want her picking up too much colour.

Perhaps because he was the first born, Dan had a rockier time with our father. Dan has no doubt that our father gave us mixed racial messages. When my brother was eleven or so, Dad gave him a stocking to wear on his head at night. The idea was to straighten out Dan's hair while he slept, or at the very least to keep it from getting too curly on the pillow. I asked Dan if Dad had told him why he had to wear it.

"It wasn't good to have curly hair. He'd pull a hair out of my head and put it on the table and say, 'See? This is curly. It's not good to have curly hair.' And I remember feeling extremely hurt and ashamed, and I started wearing the stocking cap. I remember feeling very concerned that my hair was curly, and I remember being frantic about straightening it."

When Dan told me this story, I noted the irony in the fact that a man who had devoted his public life to human rights would yank a curly hair out of his son's head and say, "Look at this. This is not good. Straighten your hair."

Dan replied, "I wouldn't say it was ironic. I find it makes total sense, due to the strange paradoxes of human nature. I think that kind of paradoxical behaviour is very common among people like our father, who have worked in the field of human rights or social work. There are contradictions. Very often, people go into these fields as compensation for their own feelings of inadequacy. That way, they can still bring those feelings of inadequacy, and guilt, and self-hatred—self-racial-hatred—into the house. They're trying so hard to do the opposite, in terms of the real world."

The mixed messages didn't come just from within families like ours. Many people I interviewed indicated that their first strong sense of racial awareness sprang from negative experiences—most often from being insulted by whites.

Karen Falconer, now an elementary school principal in Toronto, has an Eastern European–born mother who is white, Jewish, and a Holocaust survivor. Her father, a black man, is a light-skinned Jamaican immigrant. Karen and her six siblings grew up in the predominantly white suburb of Mont Saint-Hilaire, just outside Montreal, and the children's race was never discussed when they were young. Indeed, the matter was kept so entirely under wraps that one day, when she was eleven, Karen was flabbergasted to find herself being called "nigger" at school. "I would sit at the mirror and ask myself why they were calling me that." Karen hadn't known her own father, an explosives chemist, was black. Nobody had told her, and he certainly hadn't spoken about it. "Suddenly a light went on. I realized that my father was black, but I still didn't feel it was part of me."

Years later, when she was attending McGill University and dating black men, she confronted her mother over that time in her childhood. "I said to my mother, 'During all the time I was being called nigger, why didn't you tell me I was black?' And she said, 'It didn't ever occur to me.'" In retrospect, Karen notes that her parents believed that race was of no consequence. Being black or white simply did not matter to them as parents, she says, and therefore they never discussed it at home. Her mother was facing the challenges of raising Jewish children, and that overshadowed any other identity issues. "Looking back, I find it interesting that I never consulted my father at any of those stages, although, ironically, he was the one in the best position to discuss it with me because he was the black parent."

Karen notes that neither she nor any of her six siblings married a black person, and she was one of the few to develop, even for a relatively short period of time in her youth, an intense involvement with the black community. However, her brother, Julian Falconer, is now a well-respected lawyer who has worked extensively in the area of anti-racism for the black communities of Toronto. Since his early career days, he has acted as counsel to the Urban Alliance on Race Relations and frequently represented families of colour who have lost loved ones in police shootings.

Despite the fact that Karen now shows a strong sense of racial awareness, she notes, "I grew up in a family that did everything it had to do to ensure that race wouldn't be an issue. My parents were ambitious for us. They set the standards very high from the word go. To achieve those standards, in Montreal or Toronto, it was easier to be in a white world. But when I consider this now, especially as a school principal, I am filled with profound sadness that this was the truth, and hope that children today would not be confronted with the same choices. Children need the freedom to move within any racial environment, see role models succeeding all around them, and believe that their own futures are secure."

Karen now identifies as a Jewish person of colour. "I know I'm not a white woman. I can't exactly say I'm a black woman, either, because at some level I don't feel that I've earned the right to do so. I am now confronted with how much I needed to be either black or white when I was younger. However, I no longer feel the same angst. At the age of forty-six, coming up with a clear sense of racial identity just doesn't matter as much." Nonetheless, Karen has made sure that her own children know about their black heritage.

For others, early negative experiences led them to identify strongly as black. Cindy Henwood was born in 1973 in Swaziland, to parents both formally classified as "coloured." When Cindy was eight years old, her parents left Swaziland and came to Canada. A year later, the family settled in Dundurn, a small and entirely white town outside Saskatoon. A short time after arriving, Cindy found her way into a grocery store blocked by a boy who said, "There's no niggers allowed in here." It was a brutal lesson. "If you don't look white, you can't just be a Canadian," Cindy observed. "You have to qualify it, always." Her parents thought of themselves as coloured, and did not by any means self-identify as black. But for Cindy, one of the most natural ways to adapt to life in Canada was to embrace her black identity.

Carol Aylward, born in 1950 in Glace Bay, Nova Scotia, responded in a similar way to racism. Her black father had grown up in a black neighbourhood in Sydney, and her white mother, originally from Newfoundland, was of Scottish and Irish background. Her parents married in 1945. "Back then, it was a major deal," Carol said drily. When Carol's parents moved to a white part of Glace Bay to live with her maternal grandparents, neighbours tried in vain to get rid of them with "numerous petitions and cross burnings."

Carol, who is now a law professor and former director of the Indigenous Blacks and Mi'kmaq Programme at the Dalhousie University law school, was the first black student allowed into the all-white school in the Brookside neighbourhood of Glace Bay. The year was 1955, and school segregation was still permitted by law in the province. The principal, who was also Carol's teacher, introduced her to her five-year-old classmates as "the nigger of the school."

"I was treated as black from the get-go," she recalled. I was never invited to classmates' homes. They weren't allowed to play with you. You couldn't go into most stores, although you didn't have the same hassles with stores owned by Jewish people."

Still, Carol was lucky. Unlike many Canadian blacks growing up in the 1950s and 1960s, she had access to a clustered black community. The Pier, a working-class neighbourhood in Sydney, was (and remains) a largely black community. Although Carol lived in a white area, the Pier was only a twenty-minute bus ride away, and she would often travel back and forth to it to be with family and friends. "As a child, I was always accepted as black by the black neighbours. I experienced rejection only in the white community, not in the black community. You were never mixed—you were black. Your heritage made no difference."

Exposure to strongly rooted black communities is unquestionably important. And for black and mixed-race people, the lack of access to such communities can be devastating. This point was driven home to me in February 1999 when I interviewed Amanda (not her real name), a twenty-year-old criminology student in Saskatoon. Amanda was raised by two white adoptive parents, and has been told that her biological father was black and her biological mother, white. She was raised in a white community, with little or no contact with black people during her childhood and youth. "My mom was blind to the fact that I am a minority. She refused to deal with those issues." When she asked what to say when children in the playground asked about her looks, her mother advised, "Just tell them you have a really dark tan."

"My mom is one of the most racist people I know," Amanda says today. "Why did she adopt me? I don't think that she stopped and thought, I'm going to be raising a biracial child."

In grades five and six—a time during which name-calling began for many of the people I interviewed—other students started lobbing racial insults at Amanda. "Diarrhea head," "pubic hair," and "face like a monkey" were the usual ones. "I started seeing myself as black because people were constantly in my face about it," she recalled. At the same time, other people would deny that she was black because her skin was relatively light in tone. "You're not really black," they would say, comparing her to two dark-skinned black students in their school. The contradictory messages confused her, and during high school she backed away from racial issues and from any active racial identification.

"I don't know how people see me [today]. I don't have any black friends in Saskatoon," she said at the time of the interview. She said she hesitated to venture into the black community, for fear of rejection.

Unfortunately, Amanda is not alone in her experiences. If ever a person had a right to be angry about being of mixed ancestry, and to despise her own identity, it would be Sara (not her real name). Born in 1964 and the youngest of four siblings, she has lived life the hard way. Sara, who lives in London, Ontario, is a single mother who left her abusive husband when the children were young. She went on to complete her undergraduate degree in education, later obtained a second degree in journalism, and then became a school teacher. Her mother, a white immigrant from England, left the family when Sara was five years old.

"Her family gave her a choice," Sara told me, "to be with the niggers or to be with them. To be back with them, she had to abandon us." Sara mentioned that her mother came from a wealthy family, and that she had memories of her maternal grandmother calling her a nigger.

When she was seventeen, around the time that her older sister died of cancer, Sara tracked down her mother, who had moved to Toronto. They met a few times over the years, but her mother showed little interest in the relationship. Sara's father, a black man who was sixteen when he married Sara's mother, had to leave high school to support his family. He became a mechanic. When his second wife died, Sara's father had his own grandfather move in with them to help take care of the children.

"My father would say to me when I was a child that I wasn't black, that I was a mulatto," Sara recalled. Sara has a brown complexion, and her blackness is unmistakable. She was ostracized repeatedly as a child—by peers, teachers, and other adults—for being "a nigger." For Sara, the word "mulatto" denies her own experience as a black woman. "What's the benefit of my claiming my mother's white, because I'm black in the eye of the beholder? I get no white privilege. I get zero. Calling me mulatto is insulting. My dad wanted us to be different. My dad didn't want us to be black. My dad probably thought he was doing us a favour. I think my father hoped that we would have an easier life. Parents never know the complexities of that experience."

Sara is an active and playful person who loves to cook, read, work out, take the dogs for a walk, drive her son to hockey practices, and knock down and rebuild walls of her recently purchased suburban house. Her home is always full of people—her friends and those of her three children—and it's a tribute to her own strength of character that she hasn't allowed bitterness to overrun her life. Nonetheless, she shows a flash of anger when she talks about black and white people who get together and have babies without first giving the issue serious thought.

"Parents will never know the complexity of the mixed-race experience of their children," she said. "People think that the baby of a mixed-race couple is cute. 'Oh, they'll have nice babies,' people say. But it's offensive. It's not an easy life. How is it that white and black people can have relationships without thinking of the children? Do they just have one another and have a baby and not discuss it? There's a lot of bleeding going on. There are wounded people out there. It's a difficult space to occupy, being of mixed race. It doesn't mean that having two white or two black parents is necessarily easy. But being of mixed race adds another layer of difficulty. I'm not saying it's bad. But I couldn't, myself, consider having children with a white man, because I know how difficult it is."

• • •

Sara's remarks made me wonder about my own parents. Did they sit down ahead of time and discuss how they would go about raising the children of an interracial marriage? When I put the question to them, my mother said, "No, I don't think we did. I know that my brother Frank wrote before the wedding, and said that he had no problem with interracial marriage, but what about the children? I wrote back and said, essentially, that I wanted to have children, and that if you have children, then you give them love, attention and love, and that's what counts, no matter what they are. I don't think we gave too much thought to it, in terms of sitting down and having a philosophical discussion about it. I think we both thought the same way and knew we felt the same way. So that's how we went."

At this point, my father piped up. "Our kind of love," he said, "could overcome the racial barrier." I had to smile at my father, whose answer seemed to contain a mix of naïveté and determination. But there was much truth to it, because my parents have loved each other for nearly fifty years. My father was confident about his marriage from the beginning, and confident that the children would be fine. If they were well fed, well loved, and well educated, the rest would fall into place. I wonder, sometimes, how he would have reacted if I had been able, as a child, to tell him about the questions and uncertainties floating in my mind.

One time in particular stands out for me. I was about eight years old, but the memory remains clear. My paternal grandparents, Daniel Hill Jr. and May Edwards Hill, were about to celebrate their fiftieth anniversary in Washington, D.C. I worried about how my American cousins would receive me. I had already met my paternal cousins a few times. All of them were American Negroes, which was the term in vogue in those days. All of them had black parents on both sides, although a handful—and I took comfort in this—were almost as light-skinned as I was. I remembered them as bright, rowdy, playful, and affectionate, but still, as the date for the fiftieth anniversary party drew near, I wondered if they would accept me. Was I too white?

During the long drive from Toronto to D.C., I kept looking at my mother. From the back seat of the Volkswagen Beetle, I studied the profile of her face. Digging into a gravy-soaked hot sandwich in the Turkey Ranch restaurant in upper New York State, I took another look at her hazel eyes, straight hair, and white skin. My mother's skin is as white as white gets. She can't stay in the sun or she burns as pink as a lobster. I was troubled by my mother's whiteness. Embarrassed by it. Couldn't she have looked at least a little darker, a little less white? Perhaps like a southern Italian? If only she were darker—I wasn't actually wishing her to be black, just less white—then I might have an easier time fitting in with my cousins down south. Maybe they would accept me more readily.

Straight hair, hazel eyes (same as mine), white skin, university-educated, Cartesian-thinking, straight-ahead white American accent born out of the middle-class suburbs of Oak Park, Illinois (Hemingway country, by the way)—these details were making me uncomfortable about my mother on the way to the reunion. She is warm and talkative and feisty and opinionated and loving, but she is utterly incapable of folksiness. This I already knew. My father had a Ph.D. in sociology and could hold his own, in my view, against anyone who wanted to get serious or intellectual, but like the rest of my black American cousins, he lapsed into verbal playfulness at social occasions. His university education disappeared like a stone in water, and what bubbled up were hand gestures, a willingness to laugh with his body, and, most interesting of all, a new way of speaking. I'm not saying that he messed around with the down-home, illiterate-sounding blackspeak so absurdly and stereotypically presented in the media to this day. He was university educated, a professional, and damn proud of it, and if there was anything he hated it was the idea that all black people shuffled and ate watermelon and fried chicken and danced well and sang in tune and were primed and ready for sex all night and spoke in disabled diction designed to amuse and entertain whites. However, Dad's diction grew more colourful when he was with family. "Child," he might have said to my six-year-old cousin in a fancy pink dress, "you look so appetizing today that I'm about ready to eat you up." My mother, on the other hand, had no inclination to take part in this chameleon approach to language that was so common among my black relatives, and I worried that her unflinching whiteness might compromise my own chances of fitting in.

I was relieved to discover that all went fluidly at the anniversary. They served crab cakes, which I'd never eaten before, and we, the many cousins, raced around my grandmother's garden and tore up and down a forest path, doing our level best to ruin the jackets and ties and dresses into which we had all been stuffed against our will. Nobody seemed to hold my mother's whiteness against me, or my brother and sister. Mom didn't seem the least bit disturbed or insecure about her own race, and she just carried on as usual, enjoying the people in my father's family—most of whom she genuinely loved. Still, I wished I was darker. I wanted my blackness to be taken as a given, a *fait accompli*, and even though I was loved in the family, I felt somehow that I would have to affirm my racial identity to be truly accepted.

I Wouldn't Have Time to Educate Her

I have kept vigil in just about every hospital in Toronto. At Toronto General, they operated on my father's foot. At Scarborough Grace, they amputated his left leg. At St. John's, they taught him how to walk again. At Mount Sinai, they cut out his prostate. At St. Michael's, they cut off his right leg. St. Michael's, where he currently receives treatment, is an ironic but fitting hospital for my father. Ironic, because orderlies and nurses and doctors at this Catholic hospital have opened their arms and their hearts to a man who, even on his deathbed, remains an argumentative atheist. Fitting, because St. Mike's is right downtown, abutting a lovely but sad park that houses—day and night, summer and winter— a regular coterie of homeless people. The old man has spent his life fighting for the rights of people like these who, as he says, haven't a pot to piss in or a window to throw it out. In the 1970s, when I was a teenager, Dad came home exultant after a trip to Kenora, where, as the head of the Ontario Human Rights Commission, he was working with the First Nations. On a lark, they gave him a citation that described him as the best white man they'd ever dealt with. My father, Daniel Grafton Hill III, has been many things: son of a minister of the African Methodist Episcopal Church, American soldier during the Second World War, sociologist, historian, husband and father, human rights pioneer, ombudsman for the province of Ontario. But he has most certainly never been taken for a white man.

Right to the very end of his life, Dad continues to be reminded of his race. A year or so ago, a doctor he hadn't met before floated into the hospital room. At that time, Dad was recovering from prostate-removal surgery. The doctor, a youngish white man, checked out my father. "He looked me up and down," my father told me. "He checked for swelling. He rolled me over. He looked utterly confused. Finally, he said to me in a low tone of voice, 'Mr. Hill, I'm trying to understand the discoloration of your skin. Is there anything you can think of to account for it?'"

My father let out a long breath. He took another, then let that one out as well while the question hung in the air. He lifted up a big brown hand, looked over the palm and the back of it, let it drop back down on the bed. "Doctor, are you telling me that you have never seen a black man before?" The physician's jaw dropped. Dad just had to get in another jab. He reverted to obsolete terminology, to the language of his childhood, to the language that predated his immigration to Canada. "I am an American Negro, Doctor. A coloured man. Take a careful look, now. You may see some more of us out on the street, and I wouldn't want you unduly and unnecessarily agitated."

Why do so many of the stories involving Dad have to do with race? Everything about his personality seemed to reinforce his blackness, what it stood for, and what he made it stand for. Indeed, my father has always known exactly who he is: a black man. And he's always known, right down to his bone marrow, that getting a university education—a doctorate, no less—was the only way for a black man to avoid being debased in America.

Passing for white would never have tempted my father, even if his skin had been light enough for him to try. I might have been able to get away with it here and there, but I could never have pulled it off completely. And like my dad, I've never been tempted, either. My children, however, won't have to be tempted. They're going to have a hard enough time asserting their blackness and getting people to believe it.

I tell my children they're black, because they are. I also tell them they're white, because it seems an absurdity to deny it. Almost every schoolmate, teacher, and soccer coach they encounter is going to assume they are white. In a certain way, they're white because they look it, or so much so that I doubt they will be challenged much about their race. In fact, should they decide later in life to assert their own blackness, they're going to be climbing a steep hill. How ironic this is. For centuries in Canada and the United States, if you were known to have black ancestry, you were black. And that was that. The laws of slavery and segregation made it so, as did regulated customs such as where you could live, eat, work, and worship, and at whom you could direct the lustful eyeball. A plantation owner could rape his slaves and get away with it, and then turn his own children into slaves to be raped again. This barbarity was allowed, but it wasn't discussed. And a black male, somewhere between man and beast, could hurl off his shackles and rape an innocent white woman—and certainly did a few million times in the collective imagination of enfranchised North Americans. This crime was not allowed, but much discussed. Rape was either allowed or discussed, depending on who was committing or thought to be committing it. But making love across the colour line? Inconceivable.

Six years *after* my parents married in 1953 in Washington, D.C., a judge just a short drive away in Virginia convicted a black woman and a white man of violating that state's ban on interracial marriages. People these days may not appreciate the depth of my mother's courage in choosing a black man for a lifetime mate. As far as we know, there are no Africans lurking in my mother's genealogical tree, which is stocked with white Republicans. Yet the woman is just as black as my father when it comes to her ideology and her approach to life. She is seventy-three years old and tending to her dying husband, yet she still fires off angry missives to politicians who irritate her. And she actually cares enough to rail and curse when they send her back polite form letters that say nothing at all. Her husband's health is completely in her own exhausted hands, and my mother still wants to change the world. So yes, my sense of identity and my connection to my own blackness spring just as much from my mother as from my father.

Some people still squirm in the face of the truth: some black people and some white people love each other. They want to touch each other. And why wouldn't they? If we're going to run around making impossible rules, such as blacks must stick with blacks, and whites with whites, we are inviting what we fear the most. The lesson of reverse psychology is that if you want people to do something, tell them not to do it. As for the multitudes of North Americans who have laboured so frantically to shield white skin from black, what did they expect? They helped create the very sexual tension they sought to prohibit. And what have I to say to those brave souls of generations past, the men and women who crossed the racial divide at grave personal risk? To my parents, and to all others who have walked the same road, I hope the journey was rich. I hope you had some wild, gut-splitting pleasure along the way. I hope you drank every last drop from the cup of love, and that some of those drops, or at least the memory of them, stayed in your bellies for years and years and years.

. . .

When you're black and white, negotiating racial identity is like going through a revolving door. You think you're sure-footed and slipping through just fine until someone shoves the door and a big glass wall smacks you from behind and you stumble sheepishly into daylight, mumbling, "What was *that* all about?"

When I was on a book tour a few years ago, I had exactly this sensation. A white man stood up after my reading, explained that his wife was black, and announced that he felt hurt and excluded because one of his children had identified as black. "So where does that leave me?" he asked. "Who am I in this equation?" I tried to say something kind and understanding, but I doubt my answer gave him any comfort. What I actually felt was a shot of impatience. Get a grip, I thought. Get back in the real world.

This fellow irritated me because I felt his naïveté amounted to a denial of blackness. You can have a white parent and still be considered black, but you can never have a black parent and be considered white. Unless you are so light-skinned and devoid of black facial features that you can pass for white, you don't get to be white in this society if you have black parents. It ain't allowed. You'll be reminded of your "otherness" more times than you can shake a stick at. This is one of the reasons why I self-identify as black. Attempts at pleasant symmetry, as in "half white, half black," trivialize to my eye the meaning of being black. This doesn't mean I don't love my mother. I love her as profoundly as I love any person on earth. I carry her presence, her intelligence, her passion, and her empathy in every cell of my body. But I just don't see myself as being the same race as she is. In fact, I'm not even in the same ballpark. I am, however, in the same ballpark as my father. I raised this issue with my mother recently, knowing that she has no illusions on this score.

Mom is sharp-tongued, easily aroused, quick-witted, and a perfect counterbalance to my deceptively charming father. Dad is like a thief in the night. He'll pocket your sympathy and allegiance before you even know he's got them. But Mom goes for the jugular in the light of day.

"Listen," she told me, "when I married your father, I knew that our children would be black. I would have been an idiot to fail to see that. Look where we came from."

When she was twenty—this was a few years before she met my father—she stunned one of her friends by announcing that she doubted whether she could marry any man except a black or a Jew. "What white man would share the intensity of my convictions about civil rights?" she asked.

My mother, Donna Mae Hill, née Bender, was born in 1928 in Watertown, South Dakota, and lived briefly in Minneapolis before moving to Oak Park, Illinois, where she attended the Oak Park River Forest High School. At that school, there was one black student. There were no blacks in her neighbourhood, and race issues were never discussed at home. Her father was a Republican, as right-wing as you can be. He was trained as a pharmacist but spent most of his working life as a pharmaceutical journalist, and he moved his family to Chicago to take a job writing for *The American Druggist*. Mom grew up in a religious family. This fact still knocks me out. I didn't set foot inside a church until I was seventeen and travelling as a tourist in Paris. My mother and her twin sister and her two brothers, however, attended a fundamentalist Pentecostal church, and then moved with their parents into the more cerebral, socially oriented Congregational church.

When I asked how she developed a powerful racial consciousness in the household of a staunch Republican father who told jokes about blacks, Jews, and Mexicans, Mom pointed to her church, where social issues were discussed frequently. "When I was in high school, a well-placed black family, whose father had a Ph.D. in chemistry, applied to join our church. There was a lot of discord about this. Our minister finally said, 'If you don't admit them as members, I'm leaving this church.' So the family was admitted to the church and that was that."

After the Second World War, Mom attended Oberlin College in Ohio, which was the first U.S. college to admit blacks and women. Even there, she raised the roof, pushing the university administration to stop housing students according to race in the residences on campus. After graduating in 1950, she worked with a Cleveland civil rights coalition to push Ohio to adopt anti-discrimination legislation. Then she moved to Washington, where she worked for Americans for Democratic Action—a group to the left of the Democratic Party.

In her spare time, Mom did volunteer work with the Congress on Racial Equality. She was soon staging civil rights sit-ins at segregated drugstores. "Walgreen's was just one big chain of pharmacies that had what I would have called a soda fountain," she told me. "But at a soda fountain, you could buy a sandwich as well as ice cream and stuff. The idea was that we would go in, and we would wait for somebody to get up from a seat, and then one of us would sit down. We were a mixed group. We were blacks and whites. So one would sit down and wait for someone to come and wait on him or her . . . If a number of us were sitting at the counter, the employees were instructed to try to pour ammonia on the counter and wave it at us to discourage us. What bothered me was the total futility of it, you know. It was really not going to change anything, and it isn't as if we had photographers there, taking pictures and putting stories in the paper or anything. So we were just attempting to make a change and getting nowhere at all. But we were in the vanguard of what became the civil rights movement, of what everyone calls the civil rights movement, but people had been working, you know, to try and make changes long before Martin Luther King and Rosa Parks."

While my mother was trying to change the world, my father was trying to change his own small corner of it—mainly, to expand his opportunities in life. He was born in 1923 in Independence, Missouri, and lived in various other states—Colorado, Oregon, California, and Pennsylvania—until his induction into the American army. He was discharged from military service at the end of the Second World War. On the American GI Bill, he finished his undergraduate degree at Howard University and then spent a year in Norway, studying at the University of Oslo.

You can imagine the leap my father made, going from Washington, D.C., to Oslo. There were virtually no black folks in Oslo, but nobody stopped him from going anywhere or doing anything in that city. He could eat where he wanted. Sleep where he wanted. Take any bus he wanted. Date whomever he pleased. My father says that going to Oslo made it impossible for him to return happily to the United States. It became impossible for him to live in a segregated city such as D.C. After his return from Norway,

Dad gave an old army buddy royal hell for buying takeout food at a window at the back of a whites-only restaurant.

"What you doing, patronizing that place?" he asked. "Why are you giving them your business?"

"Where else you gonna get ribs like this?" his friend said.

"Plenty of places. I'll show you." When my father gave restaurants his business, they had to be either integrated or black-run. He would not stand with cap in hand at the back of a segregated restaurant. "I loved my crab cakes and my shrimp," Dad said, "but I refused to go to any restaurant that was going to make me buy food at the back door."

Washington, D.C., and my father did not get along. He had grown up mostly on or near the West Coast, where there were too few blacks to make it worthwhile for the whites to bother with segregation. He attended integrated schools all through high school, in Oregon and California, so the stratification of D.C. was a real eye-opener. Spending several years in the segregated U.S. Army didn't exactly curry his allegiance to the country. After being discharged, he and his friends would say, "The Eagle shits today" when they got GI cheques in the mail to pay for their education.

After my father came back from Norway, he floundered a bit in D.C. He didn't know what to do with himself, but he knew he didn't like it there. One day, his father sat down with him and said in a quiet voice, "Son, you are not made for this country. If I were you, I'd get out." My father applied to universities in Toronto and Mexico City, and when he heard first from the University of Toronto, that's where he headed. He did a master's degree in sociology and later completed his doctorate there. In between the two, however, he took a year off to return to D.C., live with his parents, and teach at a black college in nearby Baltimore. "I taught five courses in sociology at Morgan College for the princely sum of three thousand dollars a year," he told me. "And that was the year I met your mother."

If one perfect woman ever existed for my father, it was my mother. And if one right man ever existed for my mother, it was my father. They both had flaws—plenty of them. Sometimes they drove each other nuts. They sometimes argued like mad. But there was always love, even in the arguments. I have childhood memories of my mother standing in the kitchen and hollering at my father. While she was carrying on, he'd sneak up on her and plant a quick kiss, like a boxer with a jab, on her left cheek. She'd wipe it off and he'd kiss the right cheek, and then they'd throw their arms around each other while Dan, Karen, and I moaned in disgust. It gave us indigestion then, but it gives me real pleasure now to remember it.

When Dad met Mom, she was working as a secretary for the Democratic senator Herbert Lehman. Dad had already declared to a friend that he wouldn't go out with a white woman who was unaware of racial issues because, as he said, "I wouldn't have time to educate her."

Dad was spending the year living with his parents on Chain Bridge Road and partying it up between teaching sessions at the college. Mom was living in one of the only two racially integrated and coed rental properties in all of Washington, D.C. It was called the Friendly Co-op, located in a rundown area fairly close to downtown, at 1320 Vermont Avenue. In this dilapidated three-storey house lived men and women, black and white.

My mother had recently returned from a month-long island-hopping trip through the Caribbean, and had brought back six bottles of Mount Gay rum. "Of course, you don't drink rum like that all by yourself. My friends and I were all sitting out on the front step of the co-op, drinking rum. Dan arrived to visit a friend of his, and that was the first time he laid eyes on me. Well, he continued to lay eyes on me."

Dad countered, "I saw a very bright, very perky, highly intelligent woman. I thought she was a good-looking woman, too, with darting eyes. She had an excellent vocabulary, and I felt I could always improve mine through her. She came out of that Oberlin tradition—bright people. She came from a very intelligent family. I wanted to know what made that girl tick. She was the first Oberlin woman I'd ever dated. I'd heard a lot about that school. The first school to admit blacks, first school to admit women."

When I asked my parents if they had stopped to consider whether they were ready to jump into an interracial relationship, my father flatly said no. And my mother said, "I think we just believed that we loved each other and that was what mattered. Nothing else mattered—not race, not hostile individuals. The only thing that mattered was we loved each other."

Less than a year after they started dating, my parents announced their plans to marry. I suspect that Dad's parents, especially his mother, were secretly delighted that he was acquiring status by marrying a white woman. But one of the family friends, on learning of the engagement, said to my grandmother, "If I had known that he liked blondes [meaning light-skinned black people], I could have introduced him to some."

My mother wrote to her parents (who were divorced), and to her twin sister and her two brothers, to announce her wedding plans. The sister, Dottie, has always been my mother's closest friend. Dottie didn't oppose the marriage, but she did worry about my parents. Mom told Dottie that she and my father were going to move to Canada, where my father would complete a doctorate in sociology.

At that point, Dottie piped up with a response that has gone down in the annals of our family history: "What are you going to do then?" she asked. "Move to Sweden?"

Mom thought that her mother would support her and that her father would oppose the wedding, but the opposite happened. Her mother was aghast, and softened only over time after she met my father and came to appreciate that he was deeply in love with my mother. Her father wrote to her, saying that it wasn't what he would have hoped for her, but that he wished her the best. Later, when her brothers raised objections, her father wrote to them, too, to tell them that he had met the groom's parents, and they were wonderful people. My maternal grandfather was surely already telling jokes about blacks and Mexicans—he was telling them many years later, I can well recall, when my young ears were pricked up—but he came to love my father. I suppose Dad was "one of the good ones."

Naturally, responding to family members was not my parents' only challenge. Dad recalled the reaction of a friend—a black man and a colleague at Morgan College—when he announced the upcoming marriage. "He was a smooth-looking rascal. He dressed to a T, and the women loved him. He knew I was going out with Donna, but didn't say too much about that. But when he found out I was marrying Donna, he said, 'You didn't have to do that! You didn't have to marry outside the race. I could have found you any good-looking black woman who looked white.'"

Another friend—a black woman—also hit the roof. "I used to party over at her place," Dad said. "I drank a lot of gin over there, and I would sit down with her and her husband and watch boxing on TV. She said the same thing. 'I could have gotten you any colour you wanted within your race.' She was peeved, and she told me so. For her, it was a racial matter, totally racial. She ignored the fact that I loved Donna."

Mom, who was still working for Senator Lehman, told me she didn't get any flak at work. "The person I worked with most closely was from the South. She was shaken up, but she didn't say anything to me about it. I decided to go and tell Senator Lehman myself. He wished me well and told me he had a cousin in California who had married a black man."

At this point in the interview, Dad jumped in to mimic the classic line from prejudiced white people: "Some of my best friends are black."

Mom ignored him and continued her story. "Two days later, Senator Lehman gave me a Wedgwood china bowl and two sterling silver servers."

Reactions were muted in the interracial co-op where she lived, however. "Shortly before I came to live there, a young white woman had been engaged to a black guy. Just before the wedding, her mother arrived and talked her out of it. A black man living in the co-op had witnessed this catastrophe, and was convinced that I would never go through with it." Mom's black roommate also declined to attend the wedding because she didn't believe it would actually take place.

But it did take place. They married on June 8, 1953. They picked a Monday to keep the attendance down because my father had insisted on marrying in the smallest chapel at Howard University, where his father was the dean of theology. "I didn't want it to be a big event," my father said. No kidding. They didn't even bother with a reception. My grandfather married them, and my parents jumped in my

father's 1946 Plymouth Sedan, which he had picked up sec-
ondhand for three hundred dollars, and took off.

Their first stop was Hillcrest, my grandparents' country
home near Frederick, Maryland. My parents thought they
would be spending the night alone, but when they arrived,
they discovered that May and Dan—my father's parents—
had beaten them to the house. "We were both surprised to
see them there," Mom recalled. "They knew it would be a
very long time before they saw their son again, and they just
wanted to be with him a little bit longer. I didn't mind, but
I was impatient with the length of time they stayed. After
an hour or two, I went over and sat on your dad's lap. I
think they got the idea that it was time to go."

Boston became my parents' last stop on their trip out of
the United States. They drove there to see my mother's
twin sister, Dottie, and her husband, who now, most fortunately, is her ex-husband. That particular American wanted
to send one last ugly shot in my parents' direction before
they unpatriotically ditched their country in favour of
Canada. As the two couples were standing in line, waiting
to see a concert, Dottie's husband ran into some friends.
Thinking, I suppose, that he was clever, he pointed to my
father and said, "We brought this slave along with us."

Dad objected to that comment, and the next day he drove
with my mother to Quebec City for their honeymoon.
They returned occasionally to visit family south of the border, but they never again lived in the United States. Nor did
they miss it. Their attitude about their country of origin
was summed up in a little aphorism my father used to characterize the South: "If I had a house in Texas and a home in
hell, I'd sell my house and go home."

Don Mills, 1960s

The American writer James Baldwin said that he had to get out of Harlem and escape the United States to understand himself. Leaving his native land and living in France helped him to see himself more clearly, and to form a better sense of his own identity.

My parents felt this same need to escape the restrictions of their birthplace. For them, fleeing Washington, D.C., for Toronto was the only way to forge a life on their own terms—a life in which they would be free to be themselves and to be together. Ironically, however, the suburb of Don Mills in which they eventually settled became as suffocating for their children as D.C. had been for them.

The minute I finished high school, I left the family home and moved about as far away as I could get in Canada—settling for two years in Vancouver, where I studied at the University of British Columbia. Later, I lived in Quebec City, Winnipeg, Ottawa, France, and Spain—anywhere but Don Mills. My brother, Dan, didn't even bother to wait for the high school diploma. He checked out of school a year early, bought a home in the Beaches district of Toronto when his music career soared a few years later, and has since divided his time between that home, Los Angeles, New York, and Nashville.

The ink was barely dry on my sister's bachelor of arts degree when she caught the first plane to Europe—and stayed ten years. I didn't blame her. Don Mills had a way of squishing the black out of you, by dint of sheer neglect. As Karen has told me, "It was very clear in my mind that I wanted to be black. I always wished that my skin was darker so that I would be more easily identifiable as black." My sister was gorgeous in high school, but she had no decent social prospects there—not with her skin colour. Karen needed to break free of the conventional "no blacks around here" lifestyle that had left her feeling so confined in Canada. She landed a job as a secretary and, in her spare time, joined a subculture of expatriates living in Wedding, a run-down working-class neighbourhood in Berlin. She started hanging around Africans who had found themselves living in Berlin without papers, barely making a living but with an amazing system of community support. In their homes, on the streets, and in the black-run Café Babanussa in which they would drink and party and listen to music until dawn, Karen forged a network of black friends, and began to feel comfortable and welcomed in her own blackness.

Considering that neither my brother, my sister, nor I had ever felt comfortable or racially accepted in Don Mills, I asked my father recently what had motivated him and Mom to buy a house in that suburb, of all places, and to raise three children there. His answer was swift and unequivocal: "It was a good neighbourhood. It was described as the place to be. It wasn't downtown, but it wasn't too far away, either. And most of all, it was said to have good schools."

Don Mills represented the perfect choice for Dad. In this

predominantly white neighbourhood, his children would attend integrated public schools. I suspect that Dad had calculated our schools would be excellent because they served white children from well-to-do families. He wanted us to have that, too.

But, like Karen and Dan, I never felt any sense of belonging in Don Mills. I know people who have a deep, lifelong attachment to the place where they grew up. Not me. Although I had a good share of friends, I felt no sense of community. There were no blacks in my school, on my street, or in the neighbourhood. There were few Asians, either. Because I looked so different from everyone else, I feared that I was terribly ugly. I worried about having frizzy hair, big ears, a big nose, and plump lips. When I looked in the mirror, I felt horror and disgust. None of the people I admired, respected, or found attractive looked the least bit like me.

When I was thirteen, I took part in a road race in Toronto's High Park. My father happened to be there, and a *Toronto Telegram* reporter recognized him. The reporter asked him a bunch of questions, and finally a photographer came along to take pictures of my father and me. When the photos ran in the paper the next day, I shrank in horror. I hated the way my hair stuck out, moplike. I felt repulsed by the sight of my own thick lips. All the other runners on the sports page looked normal to me. But, of course, they were all white. In Don Mills, I didn't see myself reflected anywhere.

Don Mills was a place of variety stores, local malls, drugstores, and parks. Lots and lots of parks. The park system spread over many kilometres, and it was gorgeous, clean, and safe for running. Indeed, the parks are one of the only aspects of Don Mills that I remember fondly.

Wait. If I dig deeper, if I really excavate the memories, I can recall a few moments when I truly felt a sense of community in Don Mills. They had to do with watching my father in family situations and with neighbours.

My father had a thing about cigars and front porches. We couldn't stand cigar smoke and wouldn't let him light up in the house, but it amused us to no end that he would sit out on the porch, admiring (during election time) his lawn sign supporting the faintly socialist New Democratic Party. It was the only sign of its kind that I ever saw on our street. Sign or no sign, however, from his front porch Dad would call to all the children in the neighbourhood. I'd bet my last dollar that in the 1960s in Don Mills, Ontario, there wasn't one other family where the husband-and-father would sit outside, smoke stogies, and shout at all the girls and boys walking by. He would urge them to come up and talk to him, and stop, while they were at it, for a glass of lemonade.

"I've got a groundhog digging up my green beans, Vanessa," he would tell one. "What do you think I should do about that?"

"Put up a fence?" she would suggest.

"Fence won't do nothing, baby darling. I'm gonna get my shotgun and blast that thing to kingdom come."

"No, you're not. You won't do any such thing."

"You like lemonade? Pink lemonade, with bits of real lemon and orange squeezed in?"

"We've never tasted it like that before, Dr. Hill."

Dad would shout out for my mother to whip up some lemonade, and in ten minutes, ten children would have gathered around the porch. All white. All around this black man with a cigar. And all enthralled with his stories of wrestling crocodiles and outrunning bears and figuring out acceptable ways of deterring groundhogs from eating the beans in his garden.

My father had a phenomenally charismatic public persona. In private, if you countered him, and if you happened to be his son, you were likely to be taken out to the garage and "slapped sideways," as he called it. The garage door was closed so my mother and sister wouldn't hear. They didn't know, until years later, that the garage for me had represented a private space where Dan and I were taken to be hit. But in public, and around other people, the man had charm that turned him into a sort of guru. He knew how to motivate, to encourage, to get people to look farther and try harder. He was always telling people things such as "Why don't you go back to school and get your Ph.D.?" Or, "Why don't you go get a law degree? You're not too old, you know." Or, "Is this really what you want to be doing with your life?"

I can't count the number of people who have come to me, spoken reverentially of the influence my father had on them, and said that he turned their lives around. In public, he was always playful, cordial, easygoing, funny. He was popular, good-looking, educated, unpretentious, charming, and he never threw his weight around—unless you opposed him.

Dad became an accomplished storyteller. Dan, Karen, and I would sit at the edge of his huge bed and listen spellbound to his tall tales. Stories about shoot-outs between sheriffs and bad guys. Any story at all about a man or woman facing the threat of death by an animal, a storm, or a nasty person was a story for us. He had an incredible sense of timing; he knew just how to let a story unfold, how to make us die wanting to know how that bearded hermit on the sheep farm was going to deal with the next wolf attack.

As we grew a little older, he also told stories about the people he met at work, the problems they had, the problems they gave him. He usually had us laughing by the middle of the story. No matter how painful or uncomfortable, Dad's stories always had room for laughter.

Occasionally, we went out for dinner, usually to a Chinese, an Italian, or a Japanese restaurant, or a Jewish deli. My mother would tell us that she hadn't eaten foods like this until after university when she moved to D.C. My father, who was in our eyes the world's worst penny-pincher, would mostly tell us what we couldn't order because it cost too much. As for dessert, if the cheapest dessert was fifty cents, he'd tell us we had fifty cents each for dessert. No chocolate-covered banana sundaes for us. And he'd tell us we were lucky. In North Carolina, where our cousins lived, the first thing they had to find out if they went to a restaurant was where the emergency door was at the back—in case they got a surprise visit, mid-meal, from the Ku Klux Klan.

Dad's bed remained a place for storytelling, but the Sunday breakfast table turned into a forum for discussions about race, politics, and human rights.

One discussion had to do with Dad's early days heading up the Ontario Human Rights Commission. It was the first human rights agency of its kind in Canada, and it led the way in creating a human rights code, enshrined in law, that made it illegal to discriminate against people on grounds of race and religion. The commission is now a huge government agency, but when my father became its first director, there were just two employees—Dad and his secretary, Madeleine Smith. They worked in an office of the Ministry of Labour, in the Yardley Perfume building near Toronto's lakefront.

"I had a table in the middle of a whole bunch of other

tables on the main floor," Dad told me. "I had a phone and a desk, but no office. It was all open. George Bain, the well-known journalist for the *Globe and Mail*, called me up one day and said he'd like to come and talk to me, to do an interview. I said sure. I was delighted. I was eager for publicity because I wanted the Ontario Human Rights Commission to become known. I knew what he looked like, but he didn't know what I looked like. He came into the office, to the floor where I was located. I saw him. The door was about fifty feet from my desk. He looked at me, and then he turned around and walked out, and he never explained his behaviour." My parents assumed that Bain had decided on the spot that Dad was too low on the totem pole to be worth interviewing.

We also heard about how motivated Dad was, and how determined he was to stare down discrimination across the province. Mom recalled one day in particular, not long after the job began: "Dad phoned me early one day, said, 'I won't be home for a while, I've got a case to investigate.' He had heard someone complaining about a resort in Kingston [three hours away by car], so he just jumped in his Volkswagen Beetle and drove off to Kingston."

What I remember most of all is the humour and the warmth with which Mom and Dad told these stories. In *Bell vs. Ontario*, the only case of his to reach the Supreme Court of Canada, Dad lost. This was in 1971. Dad was arguing that a landlord couldn't discriminate against a prospective tenant on the basis of the prospective tenant's race, even if the landlord would be sharing the same living space as the tenant. The complainant in this case was black, and the landlord white. "The *Globe and Mail* came down on it hard," Dad recalled. "They wrote three editorials on three consecutive days condemning the commission." Dad had won the case in lower courts, but his arguments were rejected by the Supreme Court. "They basically ruled that a man's house is his castle, and he can do what he wants in it—even discriminate."

What the Supreme Court actually ruled was that the defendant, a live-in Toronto landlord by the name of Kenneth Bell, was exempt from anti-discrimination legislation. He was therefore permitted to keep a black man out of his house because the tenant's suite did not have a separate entrance and could not be considered a self-contained dwelling. My father made us burst out laughing whenever he talked about that ruling. I can still hear him carrying on about it: "Heaven forbid that this cuss-ugly black man would have to come in every day through the white man's door!"

Recently, I looked up the case. It was a five–two decision against the Ontario Human Rights Commission, delivered by Justice J. Martland, who summed up the facts neatly: "The complainant, Carl McKay, filed with the Commission a complaint against the appellant dated at Toronto on December 12, 1968. It alleged that the appellant 'allegedly committed an unlawful act relating to housing' on or about December 11, 1968, because of race, colour and place of origin, and set out the following particulars:

"'On December 10, 1968, I saw an ad in the Toronto *Daily Star* for a 3 room flat for rent with private bath and kitchen at 30 Indian Road. I phoned the number given and was told the flat was still vacant. The next day when I went to the address in person, I was told the flat was taken by a man I later learned was Mr. Bell, the landlord. However, when my girlfriend, Miss Nancy Sharp applied the same day after me, she was told it was still vacant. I am a Black man from Jamaica and feel that my failure to obtain accommodation was determined by factors of race, colour and place of origin.' "

I smiled, reading the complainant's letter. No doubt about it—I could see my father's hand in the articulation of that complaint. I was also amused to read the other side of the debate, coming, as the Supreme Court ruling noted, from the landlord, Kenneth Bell:

"On or about the 10th of December, 1968, when the flat was advertised for rent, two young negro men came to the house to inquire about it. I judged them to be about twenty to twenty-two years of age and thought they may have been students. I considered them to be too young and accordingly, I turned them down. I told them the flat had been previously rented because this is the simplest method and avoids discussion and argument.

"I did not refuse to rent to the negroes because they were negroes but because they were too young and appeared to be students and I do not want young men or students as tenants, particularly because the flat is not separated from my own living quarters and is not self-contained."

My parents would laugh as they told us how the story unfolded. They gave us all the details about how Dad lost on the technicality relating to that blasted shared entrance. Mom and Dad gave us all the fire and passion in their bellies, and they laughed to comfort each other. They taught us the love and the comfort of story making.

By the way, the case apparently generated significant media coverage. My parents warned me that we might be getting crank telephone calls. I was instructed in no uncertain terms to hang up if some stranger on the telephone started saying rude things to me. I don't recall fielding any such calls from strangers. But a neighbour made a nuisance of himself over the issue. He tried to berate Dad about the position he had taken in court. Dad cut him right off: "I don't tell you about your business, so don't even try to talk to me about mine."

Listening to stories of my father's working world instilled in us a measure of black pride. We also derived a sense of community connection from family moments around the television, which is odd because we weren't that interested in TV, and I didn't watch much of it. But the late 1960s and the early 1970s featured big stand-up comedy numbers by Bill Cosby and Flip Wilson. I can remember Bill Cosby doing his Fat Albert routine: "Hey hey hey, here comes Fat Albert," he would call out, mimicking adolescent voices. I locked onto Cosby's diction and playfulness like a missile on target. It was something that spoke to me, that I wanted more of, and with which I identified entirely. My whole family would be in stitches during Cosby's show. The same happened when Flip Wilson cross-dressed for his Geraldine routine, and when we would sit together and analyze *All in the Family*.

All of these television programs involved black actors or black themes. When I watched these shows, I felt alive. I felt that there were people in the world who were speaking to me. And as I didn't get very many real people speaking to me that way in Don Mills, I had to find other ways to connect with them. So I started reading. I ate up every bit of black writing that I could find. Langston Hughes—his stories, his novels, the Simple stories, and his poetry. Ralph Ellison. Richard Wright, whom I approached gingerly because my mother confessed that *Native Son* had upset her so much, it had made her vomit. James Baldwin. Eldridge Cleaver—now that cat fascinated me, especially when, in *Soul on Ice*, he speculated as to why black men and white women end up together. I read Alex Haley's *Autobiography of Malcolm X*, and had to struggle through the section of Malcolm X's life when he ardently believed that white people were the devil incarnate. I knew this to be false. My mother was white, and she was no devil.

Without knowing exactly what I was doing, I was forming my own sense of blackness and my own connection to the black diaspora by reaching into literature. Soon, this exploration blossomed into creative writing of my own. When I was fourteen, I wrote my first short story. I knocked it out on my mother's L.C. Smith typewriter. I loved the sheer physicality of typing. I loved to shut my eyes and strike the keys and slam the typewriter arm at the end of each line and roll the paper up snug against the round black platen each time I ran out of paper. I loved the feeling of typing almost as much as I loved to write. Yet I don't know exactly why I wrote this first story. Nobody asked me to do it, and it was wretched. It was about a black man in North Carolina who fled into the woods with his white girlfriend because nobody could understand their love, their need to be together. My mother, a hopeless unromantic, told me the story was terrible. I tore it up and tried something else. I was becoming a writer, automatically throwing pieces out and rewriting them until they sounded better to my ear. Interestingly, every time I wrote, my mind wandered into the lives of black characters.

Slowly, I was developing a sense of myself. Yet it was strange to grow up black, or to grow up with a slowly increasing confidence in my own blackness, when there were no other black people around. These days, I'm often invited into schools with lots of black students, and I feel a tinge of nostalgia for a past not lived. I can't help but wonder what it would have been like to have black people all around me when I was young, and to have them to relate to as friends. I can't help but wonder what it would have been like to go out with black girls, or compete in debating clubs, chess clubs, and track clubs with black kids. I can't help but wonder how pleasing it might have felt to be able to drift into a friend's home and find myself surrounded by black people. What a different life that would have been.

Allah's Blessing

Some twenty-two years have passed since my life changed unalterably upon setting foot in the French-speaking, predominantly Muslim, West African country of Niger. I am twice as old as I was then, and I still look back with awe and astonishment at the summer I spent in what was then described as one of the poorest nations on Earth.

Oddly, I decided to travel to Africa at a time when I was immersed in a distinct personal and social challenge: to become perfectly fluent in French, and to understand and appreciate the people of Quebec. I had been renting a microscopic bachelor's apartment in the Quartier Montcalm, just a stone's throw from the Plains of Abraham, and enjoying my role as the only Anglophone in a brutally difficult honours economics program at Université Laval in Quebec City. My friends were all French Canadian. In my spare time, I was devouring Proust and Hugo and Camus in French. In *Le Devoir* newspaper, ingested daily over croissants and café au lait, I followed the growing nationalistic fervor that would peak a year later in the 1980 referendum on separation. All in all, I had been consuming the French language and culture with such gusto that I proudly wrote home to my parents to tell them that I had begun dreaming in French.

And yet, and yet . . . there was another side to my identity that cried out to be explored. I wanted to go to Africa. I had read the recently published novel *Roots*, by Alex Haley, and I had been poring over black American literature for years. I had already begun to write short stories that explored, tentatively, matters of race and racial identity. The stories were duly circulated to friends and relatives before being tossed into a pile in my desk drawer, which is where they belonged. They weren't much good. But they signalled a brewing interest in my own racial identity.

None of my immediate relatives had been to Africa, and I was excited to be making arrangements to travel to Niger as a volunteer with the non-profit group Canadian Crossroads International. I was to travel with a group of six Québécois—all unilingual French Canadians—on a mission that was part cultural exchange, part tree-planting expedition. Niger is a landlocked country, mostly cloaked by the Sahara Desert. A narrow, arable strip in the south is the only place where people can grow food and other cash crops. Our tree-planting work, we were advised, would be good for the soil. The roots would hold down the earth, prevent erosion, and impede the massive desert from inching farther south.

I was as excited as could be. I started reading about the history of Niger and of French colonial rule there. I picked up a manual to learn some rudimentary terms in Djerma, the language spoken mostly in the south of Niger. And I got to know the French Canadians with whom I would be travelling. I visited them in their homes, with their families, near Magog in the Eastern Townships, in Montreal, and in Quebec City. Three of the people on the trip became life-long friends: Marie-Paule Lamarre, who at the time was a community worker with disadvantaged children in Quebec's Basse-Ville, Daniel Vézina, who worked as a librarian, and Line Mayrand, a university student. We spent a number of weekends together before the trip to Africa, learning about each other, sharing information that we picked up about Niger, and arranging to get vaccinations and to buy anti-malarial medication. By the time our Air Afrique jet was flying across the Atlantic Ocean, I knew and liked my friends quite well. But I had no idea what lay in store for me in Africa.

It was steaming hot in Niamey. From the taxi window, I looked out at the men, shirtless and muscled, digging ditches by the roadside. I looked at the endless stream of humanity on the move. In Niamey, everybody seemed to be on foot, or on a bike, or clinging to the back of a crowded bus. Girls half my age balanced platters of oranges and grapefruits on their heads. Boys lugged around piles of firewood. Men pedalled bikes with goat carcasses strapped above the back fender, or with live chickens stuffed into baskets over the front wheel. Mothers carried infants everywhere on their backs. Women braised fish and men cooked goat meat over small roadside fires. One man repaired shoes by a hand-painted sign that read, *Docteur pour les souliers*.

I wanted to get out of the taxi, away from my friends, and into this sea of African humanity. And that feeling escalated in intensity over the next weeks. We were lodged in a community centre in the capital city, waiting for the government's Youth Ministry to move us out to *la brousse*, as the outlying rural areas were known, to start planting trees. The seven of us slept on cots in a single windowless room, and as I lay there on the very first nights, I found myself drenched in sweat, unable to sleep in the ovenlike heat, and unable to stop my mind from racing. I was happy to be in

65

Africa, without doubt. But shooting out of every pore of my body was a completely unexpected resentment I felt for spending time in Africa with this group of whites. I hated walking down the potholed roads with them, amid their sunhats and water canteens and cameras. I couldn't stand being among white friends in such an entirely black country, where, I suddenly felt, a person was either black or white. No in-between states were allowed—or at least I didn't perceive that possibility, that summer in Niger. When I stood beside my friends in the market, buying bread and peanuts and fruit, or when I sat beside them in simple restaurants, sipping the disinfected water from our canteens, I felt that they were preventing me from being black. And at that moment in my life, I wanted nothing other than to be seen, understood, and accepted as a long-lost brother come back to Africa to meet his figurative ancestors. At every opportunity, I sought to isolate myself from my friends, to head off on my own, to talk with people on the roadside, or in the community centre, or on the streets, all by myself.

Across the street from the community centre, a young man named Moussa ran a roadside coffee stand. Over four stunted sticks of firewood, he would coax water to a boil (or nearly) and pour it into glasses containing curious mixes of instant coffee, tea bags, and Bébé hollandais tinned milk, which was saturated with sugar. I wandered over as often as possible to Moussa's coffee stand, where I would drink his brew, talk a mile a minute, and learn rudimentary salutations in his maternal language, Djerma. *Matinugo*, I learned to say, by way of hello. And *matafu*, to ask about how things were at home. And *banisamay*, to reply to another's question that all was well. I must have memorized twenty-five short salutations and expressions in my first two days in the country, to the stupefaction of my friends.

Looking back, I imagine that they saw something they had never expected from the quiet, easygoing Anglo that they had come to know in Quebec. They must have seen a young man transfixed by a desire to be accepted in Africa, and to inhale as deeply as he could the culture of the people around him. They must have been shocked as well to see me extricate myself from Québécois culture—into which I had thrown myself so enthusiastically—with such emotional vitriol once we set foot in Africa. What surprises me, in retrospect, is that I was well aware before my trip to Niger that many North American blacks had gone to Africa seeking some sort of brotherly, diasporic connection, and returned with complaints that they were snubbed and not accepted as being truly black. That awareness, however, didn't prevent me from feeling overwhelmed by the same desire, which was surely intensified by my realization that the people of Niger might not even recognize my light skin as being black, or that I had any black heritage. I was aching for them to see it. I was dying to be known and treated and welcomed as a prodigal son.

A few days after I arrived in Niamey, a little boy with a tennis-ball–sized hernia bulging from his navel ran up to me. I winced at the sight of the hernia, which seemed to jab at me accusingly. *I'm poor, you're rich*, it seemed to say. "*Monsieur, monsieur*," he said, tugging at my shirt. I looked at him indulgently. Would he be the first to recognize me as black, to salute me, to ask me who I was and why I had come to his country? I greeted him pleasantly. "*Donnez-moi dix francs!*" he shot back. I felt as if he had kicked me in the stomach. I shook my head sadly and walked away. I took myself once again to Moussa's coffee stand, sat with him there, and pronounced every word and expression I had picked up in Djerma. I said the words as I pointed to the goat meat over the fire, to the women with babies strapped to their backs, to the canned milk that oozed like syrup into the glass set before me. Into the glass went the dark grains of dried Nescafé, and then the half-boiled water, which made the steaming black drink swirl with creamy whiteness until it settled into brown—light brown, the colour of my own skin, which I so desperately wanted Moussa to see.

A week or so later, we were still in the city. I had made a few acquaintances, which wasn't hard, as the young people in Niger were happy to befriend North Americans. I went with some of them to a Hollywood movie, shown outdoors, and was astounded and amused to watch young men in the audience yell at the screen, hurl comments at the actors, shout their approval or disdain. One man asked me what was wrong with North American women, and why they slept with every man they could find. I asked him why he thought that to be so. "Look at this woman," he said, pointing out the main actress, who had just climbed into bed with her love interest. "Just yesterday, this same woman was in another movie, and do you know what? She was in bed with a different man!" Somebody invited me to his home, and I gladly accepted. All I recall is that we ate from a bowl of olives, and as I ate, I became aware that I was feeling unwell.

Those olives were the last thing I ate before I became violently ill. My stomach revolted, my intestines caved in, and I became sicker and sicker. I remember resolving feebly never to eat olives again. I was a thin man, but I started getting rapidly thinner. In healthier times back in Canada, I had run marathons. But being sick like this seemed more exhausting than the last miles of a race. It took a superhuman effort to lift myself off my cot and limp to the toilet, which was nothing more than a hole in the ground between two raised cement blocks. I had the awful feeling that my entire insides were draining out of me. Sometimes I felt so hot that I ached to be laid down on a bed of ice. Other times, I shivered endlessly in one of the hottest countries in the world. I knew this wasn't any ordinary flu, and I felt the threat of death.

Marie-Paule, Daniel, and Line flew to my bedside. They put wet washcloths on my forehead and changed the sweat-soaked sheets on my cot. They walked half the city to find bottled water for me, and sliced oranges to try to get some sugar into my system, but I couldn't hold down any drink or food. I heard them murmuring, gathered that they were taking my passport and wallet for safekeeping, and was vaguely aware that they were madly trying to determine whether any medical help was available, especially for foreigners. As I slipped in and out of consciousness, I heard them talking to Moussa, who had come to inquire about my health, and turning him away so that I could rest.

Two days went by. My illness got worse. I couldn't get up. They helped me to the bathroom and then into a set of clothes. My pants slid right down over my waist to the floor. They pulled my pants back up, saw that I was adequately dressed, and packed me into a taxi.

Throwing up everywhere, stumbling, unable to stand unassisted, I didn't make much of an impression on the nurses at the Niamey Hospital. Babies and children and men and women of all ages were waiting desperately for attention. Some of them had to be in situations more dire than mine; some of them would die. Dehydration and diarrhea were the most common causes of infant mortality in West Africa. Tending to me right away would clearly mean making somebody else wait too long. But Marie-Paule and the others did not let that stop them. They argued and cajoled and fought and used whatever contacts they had with the Ministry of Youth to make sure that I was admitted and treated immediately.

What do I remember of those first days? Not much. A nurse grabbed my arm and jabbed in a needle, looking for a vein for an intravenous tube. When she missed the vein and dug around for it, I howled in pain. "*Quoi*," she shot back, "*à votre âge, et vous criez comme un enfant*." The pattern continued, with aggressive nurses wielding needles that always searched before they landed. There were needles for intravenous feedings and needles for blood transfusions, and it seemed as if nothing but needles and liquids entered me during my first delirious days in the hospital. My arms were purple, blue, and black from all the needle scratchings. Things got worse before they got better, and in my perhaps paranoid state, I imagined that the nurses despised me and resented having a white man consume their rare and precious hospital resources while African people lay dying around them. The hospital had no supplies. Relatives of patients brought bedclothes, sheets, and even food for their loved ones. Family members stayed to take care of the sick. Doctors and nurses—the women among them working with babies strapped on their backs—were doing their best in a poor nation to take care of the sick and the dying. But they didn't like me. And I didn't blame them.

After a few days, as my mind cleared and my body started holding more fluids, I started thinking about my friends, who kept vigil by my bedside. They never left me alone. They lifted me to the bathroom, sometimes gave me the needles themselves, draped wet washcloths over my feverish face, and walked to the market to find bread and oranges when I was ready to start eating again. Line cooked some rice in very well-boiled water and then brought it to me in the hospital. I'll never forget that she sat on the side of the bed, next to a bag of blood that dripped into me, helped me eat, and tried to entertain and distract me by singing traditional French Canadian folk songs. I felt a love and a gratitude toward Line and the others as they took care of me. As the days went on and my health returned, I felt my soul discarding the anxious questions about my racial identity. I had more in common with Line, Daniel, and Marie-Paule than I would ever have with the people of Niger. And yet I had a family heritage and a sense of self-identity that was in part connected with the people of Africa, regardless of whether anyone else knew it or acknowledged it. I knew who I was, and I no longer felt consumed by the desire to have my identity recognized by others. I felt I had nothing to prove to anybody, and that I could enjoy the rest of my stay in Niger—and get to know its people—while developing deeper relationships with my friends from Quebec.

A week or so later, we finally made it to the tree-planting project in the rural area in the south of Niger. During the day, we planted trees with a hundred or so young men from the area. In the evening, we ate—the Québécois, small groups of the Africans, and I—from communal food bowls. Usually, the meal was millet or rice covered in blisteringly hot tomato or gumbo sauce. We ate by crouching around the big bowl and reaching in with our right hands to bring the food to our mouths. I didn't put weight back on very fast because crouching around a bowl on the ground is not a comfortable eating position. As well, the food tended to burn my fingers, and the rare, tasty morsels of meat and vegetables were always snapped up by the Africans with the fastest hands. That seemed right to me. I was getting enough food to stay alive, and I would have a lifetime in

Canada to eat well. I sensed that many times, over the coming years, I would take opportunities to meet and to eat again with Line, Daniel, and Marie-Paule. We enjoyed countless moments of talking together, working together, and watching the stars light up the night. When the rainstorms came, we would sometimes sneak out in the middle of the night, stand behind the trees, and remove our clothes to luxuriate in the cool, natural showers from the skies above. I also found time to spend with the young people from Niger with whom I was working.

Have you ever heard a donkey braying? Several desperate gasps are followed by a protracted moan that crescendoes on its way up the throat and then honks wildly through the mouth. In Africa, as I listened, I would imagine it was a mating call, and chuckle. One afternoon, I sat under a tree on a big old log, listening to the donkeys bray and chatting with a young man named Mohamadou.

Mohamadou flicked an ant off his leg and looked me up and down.

"Niger, c'est bon, n'est-ce pas?"

I laughed and told him I thought so, and that I liked the donkeys, too. Mohamadou informed me that they had donkeys *en pagaille*—in other words, tons of them. He smiled, and I noticed that his teeth were stained orange from chewing *kola* nuts. He was built powerfully, with big arms, but he did not have an ounce of fat on him. None of the ordinary rural folks in Niger that I saw had any fat. Mohamadou was known among the tree planters to be a fierce wrestler, and I teasingly challenged him to a match. He turned me down flat, saying that I was too skinny, and he had heard I had been sick recently.

"Monsieur Larry, give me your knife." He was referring to my Swiss Army knife, which he was coveting and which,

at the end of the summer, I would give him to keep. I handed it over. He pulled two limes out of a pocket.

"*Voici*," he said formally, and thrust a green fruit into my hand. "*Monsieur* Larry, may we speak between men?" He rolled and squeezed the lime in his hand; I did the same.

"Sure," I said, imagining the conversation that lay ahead of us and thinking how much my friends from Quebec would have enjoyed it. I would have liked to share it with them, but they were taking their siesta and were fast asleep at the time.

"*Monsieur* Larry, I hear it is very cold in your country, and that the white people's sun is very weak."

"Yes, Mohamadou. Canada is very cold compared to Niger. I don't mind that cold, though. The kind of heat you have here takes the strength right out of a person."

"Not me," he shot back proudly. "Is it true that white people are very weak? They tend to become ill when they come to our country, where life is not easy."

I chose not to agree entirely, which was my right by custom since I was older than my curious friend. I worded the French carefully. "No, white people are not all weak. They simply must adjust, for life is different here."

"You must roll the lime between your hands, *Monsieur* Larry, and you must press hard." Mohamadou sprawled out his legs in the sandy earth and continued. "I have heard that you have many dogs in your country."

I hummed a low note that indicated puzzled agreement.

"Aren't white people's dogs able to withstand the cold in Canada?"

"They can," I said.

He sliced off the top of his lime, the way we cut into a boiled egg in Canada, and serviced mine in the same way. Then he handed the fruit back to me with the knife. "I hear that white people keep dogs in their houses, and feed them good food, and that they love these dogs as we love our children, and that they cry and suffer when these dogs die. Is that true?"

"Sometimes, with some people. Some people become very close to their dogs."

"Close?"

"Not just white people. Black people, too. And other people. Asians, Indians, all sorts of people."

Mohamadou gave me a sugar cube, also from his pocket. "You must push it into the fruit with your thumb, *Monsieur* Larry." He showed me how to do it. And then he sucked the sweet juice that rose from the lime.

I tried, savouring the sweetness, and I heard birds in the branches above.

"There are black people in Canada?"

"Yes, many."

"Do black men take white women as their wives in Canada?" he asked.

"Some do, but not many," I said. I was ready to answer if he wanted to know more. But I was equally ready to sit there looking at the pocket of blue poking through the spaces in the treetops, thinking of the friends who had saved my life, chatting about Niger and Canada, answering the questions of this boy to whom I was distantly, deeply, simply related, regardless of whether he knew it or not.

"Do they have children?"

"Sure they do. What do you think of that?"

"You must squeeze the lime to get out all the juice, *Monsieur* Larry."

I followed his instructions and then asked again. "What do you think of that, Mohamadou?"

"Are they black or white, these children?"

"They are both. They are both black and white."

"*Monsieur* Larry," he began, pausing to watch me suck on the lime.

"Yes?"

"May Allah bless you." He stood up. "Come. The siesta is over. We have work to do now. We will plant trees together this afternoon."

Once the tree-planting expedition was well under way, I managed to remain healthy for the rest of my stay in Niger. Upon flying back to Canada, however, I chose not to go to Toronto because I didn't want my parents to see me so thin. Instead, I flew straight to Montreal and then took the bus to Quebec City, where Daniel and his family fed me and put me up until I was ready to move into lodgings for my next year at the university. Daniel's mother declared that I needed fattening up, and served me chocolate cake and ice cream until I couldn't eat any more. I felt fortunate to have travelled to Africa with Daniel because I now had a friend in Canada who knew what I had been through during my stay overseas. We have remained friends for more than two decades, and I have never forgotten the lesson I learned in Africa, as he, Line, and Marie-Paule took care of me. Like any reader of this book, I have many different sides. They all fit together into the configuration of who I am. It is possible, and indeed desirable, to welcome and nurture every aspect of my identity, and the diverse relationships that come to me as a result of living a full life. Leaving Niger some twenty pounds lighter in the summer of 1979, I felt profoundly calmer about who I was, and how I would be perceived, racially. I knew who I was, and didn't much care any longer what others thought about it.

The Same Place as Him

Last summer, my children and I were taking a boat to visit my brother, sister-in-law, and nephew at their lakeside cottage near Gravenhurst, Ontario. Bev, my sister-in-law, had come alone to pick us up and motor us across the lake to the cottage. As we neared the dock, I saw a handsome black man, middle-aged, of average height and medium build, standing at the top of a long flight of stairs. I could see his profile. I didn't recognize him. He was a light-skinned man, but definitely black, with facial features that gently underlined that fact. He had no hair, or very little, and the head was, as my father loves to say, dolichocephalic, meaning long and bullet-shaped.

As I asked Bev who that man was, the answer came to me: my brother, Dan. As he is getting older, he is even more handsome. Strangely, he looks more black now that his hair has left him and he has become relaxed enough just to be himself.

A few years ago, Sony Music Canada threw a party to launch Dan's latest CD, a greatest hits collection, and Dan and his band performed a few old favourites. I took my children along because I wanted them to see their uncle Dan doing what had made him so famous so many years before they were born.

I was stunned to see my brother walk out on stage. He doesn't perform much at all anymore, having evolved from a singer-songwriter to primarily a songwriter—for other pop, R & B, and country stars. I hadn't seen Dan on stage in years. What took me aback was my brother's face and head. I suddenly felt that I was looking at a black man. A man who could easily have been fronting a jazz band. His hair was almost gone—closely cropped to his head, salt and pepper, paper-thin. His head was lovely—again, that long, bullet-shaped, dolichocephalic form I had noticed from the boat.

Dan was clearly decades beyond the prime of his youth in the 1970s, when he walked barefoot onto the stage and sat on a stool, unaccompanied except by his own acoustic guitar. He was one helluva singer and songwriter, and a sex symbol as well with his wild beard, long and matted hair, partially unbuttoned shirts, pregnant lips. I suppose that his being of mixed race enhanced the dark, mysterious look that women seemed to find so attractive. Backstage, after concerts, they used to line up patiently to give him gifts and slip him telephone numbers. But here he was, at Sony Music Canada, a quarter of a century later—a husband, a father, owner of various platinum records, and no longer the least bit hungry for the applause of adoring fans.

He stood up on stage with a small band—a guitarist, a bassist, a drummer, a pianist—and made me think of other black singers who had gone before him, classic jazz artists such as Joe Williams.

He wasn't masking his near baldness any longer. Gone were the hats, the weaves, the desperate attempts in his thirties to make it look as if he still had a full head of hair. And do you know what? He looked much better as a result. He looked dignified. He looked like a man who was aging handsomely. And he looked black. I felt full of love for my brother. It was a damn good thing his wife was there, or some enterprising woman might have tried to jump him, take him home and lock the door.

It always seemed to me that Dan explored his own blackness through his art. Although he became a pop musician, his musical roots and influences originated at least in part from the jazz and blues singers whose voices rang out every week from our parents' record player in the living room—the central gathering place in our house. There, we watched our parents swing each other around to Ella Fitzgerald and Lena Horne and Frank Sinatra.

If Dan, as a young teen, wasn't watching and listening in the living room, you could be sure to find him in his bedroom, playing the guitar with a pen behind his ear—all the better to scribble out song lyrics as they came to him. Already, the music of our family home was sliding into Dan's soul and making itself felt in his own unique blend of folk and pop music. Dan listened back then to the Beatles, the Rolling Stones, Joni Mitchell, Gordon Lightfoot, Bruce Cockburn, Bob Dylan, and James Taylor. I remember one time, after a family dinner at the Kwong Chow restaurant in downtown Toronto, my father was driving the car and turned off the radio. But we children in the back seat were all dying to hear CHUM radio station play the hit of the week. My father said, "No more radio, I'm sick of it." Dan was so determined to hear the song that he leaped forward between my parents and switched the radio dial back on—just in time to hear Mick Jagger belting out "(I Can't Get No) Satisfaction." Now, some twenty-five years after Dan became famous across Canada and then around the world for his first megahit, "Sometimes When We Touch," I am amazed to hear the influence of black music time and time again in his pop melodies.

In some respects, it is a miracle that my brother had the fortitude to resist my father's opposition, drop out of high school, and become the recording artist that he just had to be. In those early years, when Dan was flunking math and threatening to move out of the house, Dad opposed him with all of his fury. This was the first son, after all, in a family that for generations had lived by the belief that the only way for a black person to get ahead in the world was to complete a university education—preferably a doctorate—and become a super-achieving professional. Indeed, since we were children, our father had hammered into our heads the obligation to move in this direction. We were all to become engineers, doctors, or lawyers—and we had better damn well become the best and the most famous engineers, doctors, or lawyers in Canada. Anything less than that would be abject failure. Or so my father wanted us to believe.

Dan, however, wasn't listening. He was skipping classes. He was lying about his age and dragging his guitar into bars years before he was old enough to drink in them. He would lie to my father about where he was going, what he was doing. He was as single-minded about becoming a recording artist as my father had been about leaving the United States to build a new life in Canada. There was no stopping Dan. He never faltered, even when Dad took him aside and coldly informed him that he should be "aware of his limitations," and that he would never, ever succeed as an artist. My father predicted that Dan would crawl back home broke and begging to be let in the door. Dan didn't care. He quit high school and left home. In his rage, Dad promptly converted Dan's bedroom into a home office, so that his eldest son could never return to the bed that he had known since childhood. Dan ignored Dad's fury and dived headlong into his career. He avoided my parents for a while. Within a year or so, his first single, "Peter Pan," hit the airwaves in Canada. It didn't make much of a splash, but his second song, "You Make Me Wanna Be," got a great deal more radio play. Not long after that, Dan walked back into the house with an overflowing bank account, and asked Dad sarcastically if he needed a loan.

Years have passed, and Dad and Dan get together often to swap stories. It's hard to tell, sometimes, which ones are wilder—Dan's anecdotes about the seamy side of the music business, or Dad's tales of growing up black in the United States. Dan visits Dad faithfully, often bearing gifts of jazz and blues CDs, knowing that in this time of terminal illness, music remains one of the few pleasures accessible to our father. And to this day, Dad murmurs in wonder, "I never for an instant dreamed that boy could make it as a recording star."

There is no doubt in my mind that race played into the fight between my brother and father. Dad wouldn't have harassed Dan so thoroughly if he hadn't had the experience of knowing how hard it was for a black man to succeed in North America. And Dan wouldn't have fought so hard to make it—and I have never seen a person work with the intensity, focus, and passion that my brother showed for years and years as he honed his skills as an artist and struggled to make it in the music business—if he had not been black. Our family background drove Dan to believe that he simply had to succeed. There were no alternatives.

Oddly, however, among the three siblings, Dan appears to have spent the least time trying to assert his blackness. He is black. To me, at least, there is no doubt about that.

Many of his songs touch upon aspects of blackness, and one of his most famous early songs, "McCarthy's Day," was written in the mid-1970s as a celebration of our parents' courage in crossing the colour line.

Two of the verses went like this:

Way back in McCarthy's Day
My parents left the USA—young, rebellious lovers
They left behind a nation far too proud and powerful
    to say
That love transcends all colours

And some black men turned against my father
Some white men turned against my mother
Each race has its place they all would say
And with a past so battle worn and a future begging
    to be born
They found a life that's growing still today

However, Dan never struck me as someone who had any need to involve himself "in the community," as they say. I don't think he felt a lack of identity with black people, or a lack of empathy for their concerns. He just didn't seem to need to prove anything, on that front, to other people or to himself. He simply focused on his career in music and let his social life take care of itself. When we sat down for an interview in the Sunset Grill, a restaurant near his home in Toronto, I asked Dan why his own preoccupation with racial identity seemed to fade into the background as he emerged from his teenage years.

"It just seemed to fade out of my system inexplicably, although it was probably in relation to my rising self-confidence, due to how I saw my place in the world. I was

81

developing more and more self-esteem based on my being discovered as a musician, singer-songwriter. I just naturally became more confident. And being of mixed-race identity was one of the things that put me into my own little world of creativity and left me feeling slightly different. I think a lot of people, regardless of their race, probably feel that way when they're growing up. There's a huge pressure to feel like you're fitting in—there was in Don Mills, and probably in a lot of places. I ended up almost romanticizing my mixed-race identity, and thinking that one of the reasons I had such an ability to write songs, and such an ability to sing, was the juxtaposition of the two races, and that I was a little bit like an outsider looking in. I guess at that time I felt it worked to my advantage. As I got older still, I began to feel more and more like my own person in a way that felt isolated from any kind of racial identity. I think part of that came from seeing squabbles and petty quarrels among every racial and religious group. Part of me just thought it was all nonsense, and I withdrew into my own world because I didn't want anything to do with any of it."

I mentioned to Dan that many of his songs, such as "Dark Side of Atlanta," "Indian Woman," "McCarthy's Day," and "Every Boy's Fantasy," have dealt with race and belonging, and I asked if writing them was a way to clarify how he saw himself.

"Probably part of writing is a form of self-therapy for everyone," he told me, "so absolutely it was a way of clarifying, trying to understand it better myself."

In our discussions, we were both intrigued by the fact that although Karen and I had generally thought of ourselves as black, Dan had always described himself as mixed.

"I didn't think about racial identity as much as you and Karen," Dan told me. "Probably because, though we all have our own obsessions and our own creative obsessions in a way, the music—the songwriting, and the career that came from it—was such a huge obsession for me that it overtook everything. I wasn't aware of thinking about racial identity too much one way or another. I think because I wasn't confronted with any kind of direct racism that much. I was looked upon as successful, and nothing can break through the barrier of racism faster than success. The economic situations of my life opened up such a different world, I probably wasn't forced to think about it as much."

Dan has never felt any particular longing to be actively involved in a community—black or white—and has focused primarily on his music career and his family.

I recently heard the expression "pink diaper babies," which referred to children who were raised by activist parents. Dan, Karen, and I easily could have ended up believing that the only acceptable choice in life was to follow our parents in their professional and activist footsteps. Strangely, however, while we have each been interested in matters of human rights and race relations, not one of us has become a blazing activist. And each of us has leaned more toward the arts, with Dan being the most immersed in that world.

In Dan's own way, I see him as being quietly in touch with his own blackness, and influenced by it in his reading, in his music, in the way that he sees the world, and in the way that he has helped his son David develop an interest in world issues, human rights, and racial identity.

Dan reads voraciously, and many of the books have to do with the black experience. Recently, we both enjoyed *The Greatest*, an autobiography by Muhammad Ali and one of the most fascinating books either of us had ever read. Dan has also spent his life among musicians, and he has worked with many black musicians in Canada—such as Debra Cox, Salome Bey, and Brainerd Blyden-Taylor—and in the United States. As well, I have seen Dan connect in the most intimate, playful, relaxed ways with our black relatives. I have seen their love and respect for him, and I have seen him taking it all in, breathing it, knowing that they are part of him. Dan doesn't announce or broadcast his blackness because—despite the millions of records sold, and the thousands of concerts he has given, and the hits he now writes for other recording artists—he is a quiet and unassuming man. But all you have to do is look at him stand on stage, hold the mike, sway to the beat, and reach down deep into his soul, and you can feel Billie Holiday and Ray Charles and Count Basie and Joe Williams swing out of him.

To conclude, I am reprinting the lyrics to "Dark Side of Atlanta," by Dan Hill and Barry Mann, which first appeared in 1978 on Dan's record *Frozen in the Night*.

Black man taxi driver
Takes me where I wanna go
Dark side of Atlanta
It's the only place I know
I wanna ask him where he comes from
But I'm afraid my fear will show
So I just ask him if it always rains this hard

And he mumbles back an answer
That I wasn't meant to hear
Pulls the meter forward
As if to make it clear
That there's no communication
We're both from different worlds
And all he has to do for me is drive

And I think of you so far away and alone
I wonder if the distance will make us stronger
Am I losing touch with time?
Cause still you fill my mind
I don't know if I can hold on much longer

Driver turns the corner
And sings an old blues tune
His voice so rough it mirrors
All the pain that he's been through
And I join him at the chorus
In a voice that lets him know I understand
Won't you please understand?

And I think of you the last time we made love
The newborn break of day barely breathing
And as the stars stared from the skies
We laughed until we cried
But inside I knew I was leaving

Roll down the window
My head begins to spin
Nighttime fever conquers all as the city rushes in
Eyes in the rearview mirror
They stare right through my skin
They ask me where I come from
I say the same place as him
He nods not quite believing, which is right
He smiles and tells me there'll be no charge tonight

And I think of you so far away and alone
I wonder if the distance can make us stronger
Am I losing touch with time?

Cause still you fill my mind
As my mind goes on
As my mind goes on
As my mind goes on to wander

Part Two

Border Crossings

Hair Issues

"She has hair issues."

I can't stand that sort of statement. Describing the way people think, and the worries that plague them, as their personal *issues* implies that they should buy a one-way ticket to the shrink's office and stay there good and long. But many of us of mixed ancestry do have hair issues, and to me, they reflect how we see ourselves, and how others perceive us.

When I was seventeen, I decided it was high time to do something about the wild mop that was sprouting in all directions from my head. It had become completely uncontrollable. Even when I drenched my hair with conditioner, I still couldn't comb through the knots. They shot out like a condensed, fused mass from the sides of my head. The curls had wound and twisted themselves around each other to such a degree that the hair looked like one massive dreadlock. The only time my hair looked presentable was when I emerged from the shower, soaking wet.

I hadn't been to a barber in ages and was a little unsure of where to go. I had just come back from travelling in Europe, and I was about to begin my last year in a private high school where there were no other blacks and almost no racial minorities. I felt like asserting my blackness. Making my way around in Europe had exposed me to more suspicious looks from train officials, police officers, and youth hostel operators than I had ever received in Canada. My wild hair couldn't have helped the situation. But this was 1974, and Europeans struck me as being less shy than Canadians when it came to exhibiting racial discrimination. For example, in Brussels I had gaped in shock at hand-scribbled signs outside nightclubs that said, *Défense aux noirs* (no blacks allowed), *Défense aux nord-africains* (no North Africans allowed), or other indications that blacks wouldn't be admitted unless they were accompanied by women. Some Belgian friends had tried to get me to enter the bars. "*Bof, il n'y a rien de mal là*," they would say—nothing really wrong there. But there was no way I was giving those bar owners one lousy *franc*. I returned to Toronto at the end of the summer, more feisty than usual about my racial identity.

I announced that I wanted to get my hair fixed and that I had decided to get an afro, or as close an approximation as my loosely curled hair would permit. Who helped me line this up? My white mother! In retrospect, I find this fascinating. My father, who is prominent in the black community, could easily have set me up with someone. But do you know who was cutting his hair? Corrado Accaputo, the owner of a two-chair Italian barbershop. My mother refused to set foot in the joint because it was wallpapered with *Playboy* pin-ups. My father had been going to see Corrado for as long as I could remember. And when my brother and I were children, he took us to the local barber down the street from our house in Don Mills. That barber, too, was Italian. Dan and I hated him. We came out of his barbershop looking like wannabe whites, with our hair plastered down over our heads with water or grease, and combed pancake flat. Of course, the flatness would last approximately thirty minutes—the time it took us to get home, go outside to play, and discover that our curls were beginning to reassert themselves, gesturing up like random weeds. So when my father heard that I was planning to get an afro, he suggested Corrado Accaputo one last time and then fell silent.

My mother called up one of her closest friends, who was a black woman, and came up with Cliff's Place. Cliff ran a salon on the north side of Bloor Street, near Sherbourne, in an area now dominated by high-rise buildings. My mother offered to take me there, but I declined firmly. I was grateful she had found a place that, according to her friend, was likely to do a good job with my hair. But there was no way that any white woman, mother of mine or not, was going into Cliff's Place with me. The one thought that made me sick with worry was that Cliff would mistake me for a white boy trying to be cool, slumming in a black hair salon. No sir, I wanted him to know that I was black. I wanted to be seen and recognized as black, and treated as one of the race.

On the day of the appointment, I took the six steps down from street level into Cliff's Place. A black man, still in his twenties, smiled at me. I introduced myself and gave him the standard white handshake. I wasn't getting into any kind of soul shake because I would have felt like an utter fake, and would have betrayed myself as one, too. I smiled, and so did he. I felt about one hundred degrees more relaxed and sat down to wait.

When my turn came, he took my hair in his hand and said, "Man, you can't let your hair go like this again." I asked him to work out the knots, cut a whole lot off, and pick out the rest into an afro, if that could be done.

"Sure, my man, I can do that," he laughed, and set to work. It took him an hour to go through my hair. He grumbled a little, but in a good-natured, teasing way, and had emptied the better part of a bottle of conditioner onto my head by the time he had finished. Finally, he could run a comb all the way from my scalp to the end of my hair. My hair was so long that strands could be pulled down over my forehead and past my chin. The rest was easy. He cut it and combed it out with an afro pick. My hair actually held together in a loosely curled rounded ball.

Cliff sold me a pick and told me to be sure to use it every day. "Just like your teeth," he said cajolingly. "Whenever you brush your teeth, pick your hair. You can pick it right in the shower, after using conditioner, to get through the knots before they stick together. Come back again, man, but just don't come back with hair like that. That was a lot of work." He charged me a ridiculously low rate. I gave him a big tip and left.

That was on a Saturday morning. Two days later, I was back in school, knapsack slung over my shoulder, when David, one of my classmates, sidled up.

"Larry, what did you do to your hair? You look like a goddamn French poodle!"

First, I told him to get lost. Then I said, "This is an afro. Don't tell me you don't know what an afro is. Open your eyes, man. It's how black people are wearing their hair."

"Black! Larry, you're not black. Look at your skin. I just came back from Florida, and you're barely darker than I am."

I told him that he was an idiot, and that he had no idea

what he was talking about. I felt no desire to educate this kid, who was brilliant in math but had his head in the sand when it came to thinking about the world. I walked away and resolved not to talk to him again. Yet somehow, moments of conflict like this had the effect of confirming my own sense of blackness. I knew that I could never inhabit David's world or see it the way he did. I wasn't white and never would be. But black? That I could be. That I could become. Confrontations like the one with David made me want to read black literature, seek out black people, and keep my afro.

• • •

After high school ended, I lived, worked, and studied all over Canada. For ten or so years, I lived variously in Vancouver, Calgary, Gull Lake (Saskatchewan), Winnipeg, Toronto, Ottawa, and Quebec City. Yet no matter where I lived, I never looked forward to getting my hair done. For some years it seemed that my poor hair limped from one near butchery to another. I tried one or two other black hair salons, and the people I encountered in those places always tried to cut my hair with electric shears, as they would do for black men with tightly kinked hair. My hair came out looking as symmetrical as a patch of weeds. I tried a bunch of white hair salons, and one or two of them brought out electric shears, too, until I finally began to insist from the start that the stylist use scissors for the entire job. I learned to run if anybody brought out shears.

After several false starts and wretched haircuts in Oakville, where my wife at that time and I settled and started raising children in 1990, I finally found an inexpensive Portuguese hair salon that would cut the hair of my three children for an incredible fourteen dollars, and throw in a cut for me for another few dollars. They actually managed to make my hair look decent, and I was a customer there for several years. They were kind to the children, and the cost was as cheap as could be, so I saw no reason to switch. One day, however, after my divorce, I was sitting in the hair salon, looking around, and I suddenly asked myself, What am I doing here? It struck me that although the Portuguese ladies were pleasant, I had been avoiding my own identity by going there so long. As a result of the divorce, my life was turning in a new direction, so it was perhaps understandable that I resolved once again to find a black hairdresser.

First, I walked into two black hair salons in downtown Toronto, but I got the cold shoulder in both of them. The stylists took their sweet time coming to meet me, and they gave off vibes that said, in every way but verbally, "We don't want you here, but if you insist, we'll take your money and do the job."

So I kept looking for a place. Eventually, a friend recommended a woman named Movita, who ran a hair salon near York University. I had my friend ask Movita if she could work with lightly curled hair like mine. I expressly wanted to know if she would use shears, and was relieved to hear that Movita had split a gut laughing and insisted that she was not going to use shears on hair like mine.

Movita runs the place with her husband, Ray, and they made me feel at home immediately. In fact, I felt so good about going there, hanging out with black folks, and getting my hair done right, that I arranged to bring my children back a few weeks later. I like the fact that they are now getting their hair done by Movita, too. It gives my children a rich point of contact with people in the black community.

For me, going to Movita's feels like going home, and I won't be leaving home anytime soon.

. . .

Some of the people I interviewed had great stories about their hair. For example, when Ivan Gibbs of Montreal decided that he'd had enough of a white private school and wanted to connect with the black community in Little Burgundy, one of his first acts was to get his hair fixed up.

"I used to have my hair like a white rocker's. It was really curly, but I had it down so I looked like a head banger. Then I went to a barber shop in Little Burgundy called Tough Cuts. The [black] guy who was cutting my hair said, 'Man, you look like a white boy. Gotta change that up.' He gave me a fade: all around, cut the top, got rid of the front, the bang thing, a box cut [hair on top but shaved short on the sides and back]. I liked it a lot. I said, 'Man, I look black now.' I started renting black movies, changed my music completely. I got rid of all my heavy-metal tapes, all my rock and roll tapes, replaced them with NWA, Public Enemy. It was rap, it was hip hop, that's who I wanted to be at the time."

Jody Warner, of Toronto, noted that she had started taking her young children to a black hairdresser, but that she would never let her five-year-old daughter get her hair straightened. "I think that would send her the message that there is something wrong with her hair, and that she should try and imitate hair that's not truly hers." Jody went on to express dissatisfaction with her daughter's black dolls. "You can't find a black doll with curly hair. They all have straight hair."

My sister, Karen, also expressed concern when her daughter Malaika—who was eleven at the time—wanted to get her hair straightened with an iron. "I said to her, 'You've got beautiful curls, and I don't want you thinking that you have to have your hair straightened like a white girl.' But Malaika persisted, and Karen relented. "It's like makeup. You can have a lot of fun with it, if you don't take it too seriously. So she had it ironed out that time. I was against it at first, but it's funny—she really looked nice."

Being of mixed race and having a black daughter, Karen was concerned that she didn't know much about managing black hair, and didn't know how to braid or cornrow her daughter's hair. She worried about bringing on the wrath of black women who might criticize her mothering skills and say, "You can't even dress her up. Didn't you ever learn to do your daughter's hair?" She told me, "A lot of white women with black kids feel that way, and I think it must be pretty hard sometimes when you don't know about black hair and haven't had any experience with it."

Karen tries to have fun with her own hair, and spent one New Year's Eve getting her hair twisted into two hundred braids in an African hair salon in Paris. "It was one of my first experiences being around a lot of African women, and they were very surprised to see me walking in there. Of course, my French accent was very different from theirs. I sat there and was expected to work, too, as in 'Hold this, hold that, do this, do that.' They had two or three people working on my head. I have never had so many braids in my hair as those women put in. And they did it in four hours flat, which is no time for the number of braids I had. I enjoyed the whole social experience of getting my hair braided and getting to know some African women."

But Karen also noted that it was a lot of work to take care of black hair. "You can't just step out of the house. You have to braid it, tie it, put something around it. You see a lot of women doing wraps [covering their hair in cloth] because that's a great way of dealing with your hair when it is unmanageable."

Karen observed that hair and how it is worn can take on overtly political dimensions in the black community, and Stefan Dubowski, a journalist who lives in Hamilton, Ontario, emphatically agreed.

Stefan decided some time ago to have his hair dread-locked, although he has no particular interest in Rastafari-anism. His father is of Ukrainian background, and Stefan laughed at my teasing suggestion that he might be the only Dubowski in Canada who wears his hair in dreadlocks. Once or twice a year, Stefan shells out up to a hundred dollars to have a fellow called Dreadmaster Drew—who works out of his home on Richmond Street in Toronto—pull, twist, weave, and knot his hair.

Stefan doesn't identify with black culture or hang around with black people. He likes his hair in dreads because he enjoys the style—period. He noted wryly that blacks are sometimes disappointed to find him unengaged in their politics. "The assumption is that you are soulful, politically minded, in tune with what is going on with the race."

Stefan pointed out that hair issues can become spiritually and politically charged, and suggested that the preoccupations were exaggerated. "I don't care. I'm going to wear my hair in dreadlocks and tell people it's just a hairstyle."

He admitted, however, that life isn't really that simple. "A few weeks after I got my hair done in locks my landlord came and knocked on my door. He said, 'I'm sorry to bother you about this and I know it's completely unfounded, but one of the neighbours is complaining about the smell of drugs coming out of your apartment.' One week I'm just some guy and the next week I get dreads and suddenly I'm taken for a drug dealer who is smoking pot all day."

When Sara, the anonymous interviewee from London, decided at the age of twenty-six that she was fed up with her own hair issues, she dealt with the problem by shaving her head bald. She has kept her head shaven for about ten years now.

"When I decided to shave my head, I did it just to see," she recalled. "Just to bend my gender. It was just an experiment. I realized how much femininity is tied up in hair, and that women in general—not just black women—have a lot of issues about their hair, and what makes them more feminine, what's more pleasing to men. So there was that to think about. And I just thought, There's no way in hell I'm going to grow my hair so that I can be more girly and more guys will like me. That's nonsense. They can like me for who I am, whether I have hair or no hair. What if I underwent chemo? Look at the poor women who make that transition, especially if they've lost a breast, and they're struggling with that femininity and their sexuality, and then they lose their hair on top of that, which is more femininity and sexuality. It's amazing to me. It's amazing that we can be so shallow, or that hair translates into being so much."

Sara finds that her baldness provokes strong reactions. "People questioned my sexuality, so I overcompensated by wearing a lot more skirts, makeup, large earrings. I wanted to be feminine, I wanted to assure people that I was a good heterosexual girl. But I got over that.

"White men in particular make lots of offers, inappropriate comments, sexual come-ons. They wouldn't like to take me home to their mother, but maybe they'd like to have some fun with me. I've had white men comment in disgust and yell across the street, 'Who do you think you are? You think you're a woman?'

"And while visiting Detroit, I had an experience with black women in a mall. They sort of swarmed me. There were four or five of them. . . . They swarmed me and were saying obscenities such as, 'Who the fuck do you think you are, doing that to your hair?' "

When I asked Sara what she thought had sparked the anger of the women in Detroit, she said, "I can only speculate. But black women spend a lot of time on their hair, a lot of time trying to grow it, 'cause it doesn't grow rapidly. . . . A lot of their identity is tied up in their hair, and they often do very unnatural things to it to gain some type of acceptance in the world. Seeing me, it's as though someone's spitting in their face. *Gee, I spend all this time, and look at her. Who does she think she is?*"

Sara has a Guyanese friend, a woman with very African features, who has a bald head and doesn't attract such negative attention. This fact has led Sara to guess that the reactions she elicits stem in part from her light complexion. "I think that my appearance plays on a lot of nerves. It has to do with my hair, complexion, and bone structure. And those are all sensitive issues in the black community. I'm always positioned on a peripheral level in both communities. I'm not accepted by the black or white community. I'm black in the white community, but I'm not black enough in the black community. I'm an interloper."

Cindy Henwood, who moved from Saskatoon to Toronto in 1999, echoed many of Sara's remarks in her own interview.

"One of the first things that I noticed when I came to Toronto was the wealth of beauty-supply stores and hair salons," Cindy told me. "I was coming from a place that had two hairdressers in the entire city that did black hair. They couldn't stand each other, so you either had to go to one or the other, and you couldn't let on that you were cheating. So I was absolutely thrilled to come to Toronto. I was in my glory.

"Why is hair a big deal? I think it's one of the primary things that you're judged by in terms of beauty standards. I think that from the time you're a little girl, you see that a lot of media coverage focuses on the traditional North American view of what is beautiful, and that has always been long, probably blond, flowing hair. As little girls we see that in books, we see that on television. It's very clear to us, I think, at a young age, that long, flowing hair is what is considered to be beautiful. It's very difficult for most black women to achieve that look without spending countless hours in a beauty salon or spending a lot of money on buying fake hair. So I think it's a source of a lot of pain for a lot of young black girls or girls of mixed race. Although I would say that for girls of mixed race, it's a little bit easier to achieve that look. In the black community, a lot of mixed-race girls are considered to have 'good hair,' which is longer hair, the texture not quite so 'nappy.' Black men perpetuate that idea and go after the girls with the long, straight hair."

I pointed out that Cindy's hair was long and straight and flowing around her shoulders.

"But I've been told many times that I have good hair. I have good hair because I can do this if I straighten it. I use a flat iron on this, which is a very, very hot iron that's flat and designed to make hair straight. It presses it straight. You can do that or you can use chemicals to straighten it as well. I used to use the chemicals .... We used to use them at home. We'd sit, get the hair parted, and put the relaxer in it.

Either my aunt or my mom would do it. We'd sit for hours and then put the big rollers in the hair and sit for hours under the dryer. The combing was a huge deal. Just trying to get the comb through the hair when it's natural and it's not straightened is very painful. You sit there and fight back the tears and just grin and bear it. It's like a ritual thing. Despite all of this, despite all the hours I spend in the salon enduring the heat of the dryer and the hot irons and the hours of waiting in the salons because they usually over-book, I'm still told over and over again what beautiful hair I have, how I have good hair . . .

"With older women, absolutely, there's a huge aversion to having their hair any other way than straight, using the big curlers and doing what is called a wrap, which straightens it . . . But I think with a lot of younger kids now, it's 'in' to look more ethnic, so the big afros are back, the tight curls. It's part of pop culture, it's part of the style."

Cindy also mentioned that going to hair salons can easily eat up half a day. Because she has a job as a teaching assistant at York University, she brings papers along to mark while she is waiting. Her hairdresser encourages this. "It's a very positive experience in a lot of ways. It's a bonding thing. I don't know how to describe it exactly, but it's a very comfortable space to be in, especially for me just coming to Toronto. I feel like it's my family, and you get to know everyone in the salon. You get to know their history, their families, their stories. A lot of them bring their children. It's a big social gathering and it's relaxing. It's comforting.

"The second they touch my hair, hairdressers know that I'm mixed with black. In my experience, a lot of hairdressers will come right out and ask, 'What are you?' Some of them almost immediately need to know what I am mixed with. I'll say that I'm mixed with black and white, but I'm not biracial, and then it comes up and I'll tell them the whole story. Most of the time I'll go into more detail, but then they're more willing to talk about themselves as well. It really is sort of a bonding thing with your hairdresser and so I don't feel put off by the question. You end up sharing a lot of things with your hairdresser. It's a very personal relationship. You're trusting her with something that is quite valuable to you, which is your hair . . .

"One thing that touches me is when I see how little black girls, little biracial children, are so attuned to the hair. I've seen it so many times in the salons. One time, a girl was having her hair cut because it had been damaged by relaxers. It was a traumatic experience for her. She broke down and cried. She had all her cousins and her friends in the salon. The stylist pulled them all aside and she told them, 'Do *not* make fun of her.' The girl sensed that this was something that was going to make her ugly.

"I was visiting a friend some months ago. He is a black guy and he's married to a biracial woman. They have two children together, and the little girl is turning three. The little girl is already very into hair and nails, and she loves her clothes and her shoes. I remember sitting in the living room playing with the girl, and her dad came home and he was in the kitchen, and the girl wanted to comb my hair. The little girl has tight, kinky hair and it was braided in cornrows. She was combing my hair and trying to style my hair. She didn't speak very much, but she said to me in her own little way that she wanted her hair taken out of the braids. She wanted me to comb her hair. So I asked her mom if that was okay, and she said that it was fine, so I started to undo the braids, and her mom came down and helped me take the hair out. Because her hair was very kinky, it stood up all over the place. Her father came into the living room to call us for supper, and he looked at the girl and asked the mom, 'What are you doing? You took her hair out? She looks like a Brillo pad.'

"The little girl's face fell. I have never seen anything like it. It fell, and she just sort of touched her hair. I don't even know if she knew what a Brillo pad was. But she knew that her father did not like the way that she looked. He found it ugly. It was the saddest thing I'd ever seen. It broke my heart. Her little face just fell. These things happen. You're celebrated for having the good hair. You're not directly told that you're ugly, but it's very clear that if you don't have the good hair, you're not considered to be beautiful or attractive. It starts at very young ages.

"Men perpetuate these values, too. My boyfriend is a great example. If I go to the hairdresser and I trim my hair a quarter of an inch, he will notice. He'll say, 'Why are you cutting your hair? You don't need to cut your hair.' My dad is the same way, and my brother."

Cindy wound up the discussion about hair by emphasizing that for the most part, she has felt secure about her racial identity—and how others would perceive it—in black hair salons. "Once they know that this is who you are and this is how you feel about yourself, it's sort of an all-encompassing acceptance. It's this big, warm embrace, and it's a comforting place to be. I can't think of another place or space that is like that. I know that when I'm upset, when I'm lonely, when things are getting me down, that is the place I want to be. In the salon with those people."

What Are *You* Doing Here?

If you're black and you grow up in North America, part of your very socialization process prepares you for encounters with racism. You know that once in a while, and maybe more often than that, some fool is going to call you a nigger, turn you down for a job, refuse to rent you the first floor of his house even though the vacancy sign remains in the window, pull you over to the side of the road and demand proof of ownership of that sleek car, or raise the roof when it becomes known that you're chasing his daughter.

You know you will encounter racism and you even come to expect it. When it happens, it's irritating as hell, but you deal with the situation. And often the very incident has a way of confirming your blackness, of making your racial identity real and palpable.

In 1971, at the age of fourteen, I entered a private, almost exclusively white high school called The University of Toronto Schools. The first day or two of school ran by for me much as they did for all the other new students. I found out that I would be studying Latin and philosophy—new subjects for me—in the first term. I bought my books at the textbook store. I learned, to my horror, that swim classes were mandatory and would be conducted in the nude while our gym teacher watched us bobbing and turning and thrashing in the water. I signed up for the debating club, the chess club, and the cross-country running team. And then came music class.

I came from a musical family. My parents had played jazz and blues in our living room throughout our childhood. My older brother, Dan, was en route to becoming a famous singer-songwriter. I had already played a bit of piano, taken classical guitar lessons, and studied the violin. I wanted to keep playing the violin, but the music teacher informed me that the school had no string instruments and that I would have to choose a wind instrument. I told him I wanted to play the saxophone. My music teacher cleared his throat. He straightened his shoulders. He summoned what I judged to be an exaggerated and pompous British accent, and told me that Negro people didn't have the correct facial structure to play the saxophone.

I was stunned. The air hung between us as still as could be, and I stood motionless. I resolved not to move my lips or cheeks and to hold my eyes locked onto his. I dug way down deep to show absolutely no reaction. I wanted my silent refusal to engage in any way to derail him, unnerve him, or least make him hear himself as he mumbled nonsensically about how Negroes who did take up the saxophone invariably ended up producing music that was fuzzy and sloppy and lacked clarity. *Fuzzy.* I focused on that stupid word and kept staring at him.

I wanted him to hang himself with his own words. I didn't give him an inch to move. I did not mention that I had grown up listening to jazz music, including great licks by amazing black saxophonists such as Illinois Jacquet, Coleman Hawkins, and John Coltrane. I merely pushed forward as if I had not heard my teacher.

"I have decided to play the saxophone this year. The alto saxophone."

He let out a long and painful sigh, some of which was high-pitched air pressure released through the nose, but said no more about it. I grabbed a saxophone as the first class began, and that was that. I began to learn the instrument under this teacher's tutelage.

I signed that saxophone out over and over that year, dragging it along for the hour-long bus ride home and bringing it back to school the next morning. I worked at it feverishly, but to no avail. I seemed to have no air in my lungs and no ability for the instrument. If it hadn't been for my idiotic teacher, I think even back then I might have savoured the anti-stereotype—here I was, black and useless at the sax. I did stick it out for the whole year, however, and managed to squeeze a C+ out of the class, which was a miracle in itself. I never picked up the saxophone again.

As I look back on that incident, I note that part of me welcomed the offensive remark from the music teacher. It confirmed my own racial identity in a school where I had imagined it would be lost, or blotted out, or ignored. For me, the incident and especially my quiet resolve to forge ahead contributed to my sense of self. I was able to walk away with the quiet observation that I had stood up to a racist teacher and prevailed.

For many people with one black and one white parent, it appears to hurt more when we are rejected by the black community than when we are discriminated against in the wider community for being black.

Ivan Gibbs, who was born in 1975, was put through the

ringer when he was an adolescent attending a primarily white, private boarding school in Quebec's Eastern Townships. He was called a nigger repeatedly, beaten up, left to eat alone in the cafeteria, and generally made to feel entirely unwelcome. After two years at the school, he persuaded his mother to let him transfer to a largely black inner-city public school in Montreal. There he formed attachments with other black teenagers and began working as a volunteer at the Negro Community Centre in Little Burgundy. But he recalls that the ultimate insult at the time was for a black person to call him "white boy."

"These were the people who were my friends, who identified with me, who embraced me after all that abuse at the private school, so that's why it hurt more coming from them," he told me. "You are trying to figure out who you are, hanging out with black people, and already I'm mixed, so it's harder for me right away ... But you have people saying that you're black, so you start feeling comfortable saying that you're black, acknowledging that you're black. Then you have some people who say you're not black, you know? And it's difficult, especially when you make the choice that 'Yes, I am black.' So I said, 'That's it. I'm not going to be involved with white girls. I guess if I date black girls, I'll seem more black.'"

Ivan's story is all too familiar to Cindy Henwood. "Some of the most painful experiences that I've had have been with black people not accepting my blackness or not knowing," she told me. "I feel a great deal of pleasure when a black person automatically knows that I'm black. I can think of countless times where I've assumed that everyone around me knows that I'm black, and then something will slip out or someone will ask a question, and I realize that they don't know. It's a very disarming feeling, having that sense of belonging taken away from you all of a sudden and having to remind yourself that they don't know. It depends a lot on who you're with. When you're with a group of black people, and they know who you are and they've accepted you for who you are and you can be yourself, you tend to forget that other times you'll be with a group of black people and the exact opposite experience will happen."

Carol Aylward was present at the scene of the very kind of rejection Cindy described. She had been attending a meeting just for members of the black community in Nova Scotia. Shortly after the meeting began, the light-skinned child of a darker-skinned mother was asked to leave. Carol decried the incident and any similar attempts to exclude light-skinned people from the black community. She told me that it created disunity among blacks and denied the deeper meaning of what it is to be black. "To define blackness by skin colour is not to the benefit of the community," she said simply.

Defining blackness by skin colour wouldn't have been to the emotional benefit of the girl who was kicked out of the meeting, either. I imagine the anxiety that this girl must have felt in subsequent encounters with black people.

Ironically, Carol—who is a prominent member of Nova Scotia's black community—found her own blackness being denied once during a trip to the United States. She was travelling in New Orleans and was picked up by an old black taxi driver, who asked, "So what are you?"

"I'm black," she told him.

"No, you're not."

"I am."

"No, you're not. In Louisiana, you wouldn't be black. You're too light skinned."

Carol recalled, "In the world of this cab driver, I would

never have been accepted into his community." There were two prongs of irony to this cab driver's declaration. The first, of course, was that he had denied the racial identity of a woman who had been treated as black throughout her life. The second was that his denial took place in New Orleans, where in times past light-skinned black women known as quadroons were kept and housed by monied white men.

This idea that mixed-race people are somehow not "real" blacks has put a lot of people on edge. One mixed-race woman I interviewed, and who demanded anonymity, backed away from years of work as an activist in Toronto's black community after being told too many times that she wasn't black enough to be trusted and respected.

My sister also related the anxiety she has felt about having her own blackness denied.

"I think a child deserves to have a sense of who they are, a sense of belonging to that community," Karen explained. "I mean, I grew up in Don Mills. Everywhere around me is white, and I don't have to worry about how I'm going to fit in there. I *do* have to worry about how I'm going to fit in as a black person, and how I'm going to fit in with other black people.

"When I walk into a new situation with a majority of black people, I'm much more on edge than walking into a totally white world. I feel like I'm not totally at ease in my skin. I guess I don't always feel as comfortable. I feel nervous. I wonder if people are going to accept me, or are they looking at me and saying, 'Oh, here comes a light-skinned person again, and what does she have to do with all this?'

"When I came back from living in Berlin and got a job [as a public servant] with the City of Toronto, one of the first things a black co-worker said to me when we started talking about race was 'You're not black.' We were standing at the photocopier in the back of the office, and I'm not even sure how the race thing came up. Maybe something about my father, but no, I don't even think that Dad entered into it at this point. It was later that everybody knew who he was. Anyway, we were talking about race, and I said that I considered myself black, or maybe she asked what I was, where I was from, and I said, 'I'm a black Canadian,' or something like that. She basically looked at me and said, 'You're not black. What are you doing calling yourself black?'"

As I interviewed people for the book, I was astounded to find how often those with one black and one white parent expressed a desire to appear more black, and a wariness of being rejected by black people for not being black enough.

Cheyanne Gorman, of Sydney, illustrated this point when she told me, "My grandmother always said, 'When white people look at you, they're never going to see white. They're always going to see black. Therefore you're black.'" Nonetheless, Cheyanne recalled that she was anxious, and concerned that black women would be thinking she was there to steal their men, while attending a New Year's Eve party at a black club in Halifax.

Natalie Wall, of Toronto, mentioned that she had attended a few Nation of Islam meetings in Toronto as a teenager, and heard people around her muttering and complaining about the number of "mulattoes" in the room. She complained about the degree of colour consciousness in the black community, and recalled that a woman had once approached Natalie's black boyfriend and said, "You need a dark girl in your life, you need a real Jamaican to do your cooking."

Nicole Virgin, of Mississauga, has a black mother and a white father. She likes black music and prefers black clubs when she is going out. But she dreads going, even though she carries through with it. "Someone is going to think, 'Who the hell is this white chick, going after our black men?'" One of Nicole's cousins cut her to the quick one day when he told her that because she was light skinned, she would never be seen as anything other than a showpiece on the arm of a black man.

When Nicole goes to clubs with black friends, she sometimes hears them cutting down white women. "They'll say, 'Ah, look at the slut, look at that girl.' I think, 'Wow, there are probably other groups of black women here who, because I didn't come with them, are saying the same thing about me.'"

In *Who Is Black? One Nation's Definition*, F. James Davis contends that "the lightest mulattoes" feel pressure to prove their blackness. "Since the 1960s, light mulattoes who have been put on the defensive by vigorous expressions of black pride have been made to feel that they must take pains to emphasize their respectability and their blackness or they will barely be tolerated in the black community."

I know some light-skinned blacks—some mixed race, some not—who are terrified of attending social functions in the black community. Their fear has nothing to do with their politics—the people I'm thinking of are no less militant, progressive, or mindful of the needs of black people than others attending such functions. Indeed, some of us feel that we have to involve ourselves actively in the community to prove that we belong. It is as if we expect, at every turn, some person to challenge our identity or our right to be there. And we labour under the illusion that being actively involved in the community—doing volunteer work, for example—will somehow shield us from that challenge. But all too often, we discover that no amount of volunteer work, no number of external activities, will protect us from such attacks, or prepare us for them, or prevent us from fearing them.

In 1999, I was invited to give a reading at the Over 60 club in Toronto. This club comprises black men, mostly over the age of sixty, who live in Canada. Visiting relatives and friends from other countries are always welcome. Basically, it's a fraternity of black men who meet once in a while to eat, drink, tell jokes, and listen to invited speakers.

I was tickled pink to be invited to address this club. To me, it was more than a chance to read from my latest novel. It was a welcome from the community, a sign that said, "You belong, we're proud of you, and we want to claim you."

I was given a long introduction, which began, as it unfailingly does in the black community, with these lines: "Our speaker tonight is the son of a very prominent Canadian, and an important leader and source of inspiration in the black community." I smiled through these words, felt the genuine fondness that this group of men had for my father, and walked to the mike. I gave the best reading I could, and then we tucked into fried chicken, ribs, baked yams, and peas and rice. The long evening filled with drink. The men were getting happier and increasingly rowdy. Nobody showed any sign of wanting to get up and go home.

Around midnight, I got ready to leave. I noticed that a stranger had come in the back door—a black man. He had faded jeans, an antediluvian coat, a day or two's stubble on his chin. Clearly, he was not one of the guests. I saw him studying me as I moved toward the coat rack where he stood.

"Some party," he said to me. "Never saw so many black people together in this neighbourhood. What the hell are *you* doing here?"

I looked at him. I stared. I felt ready for this guy, perhaps because I'd been talking all night. I waited a moment as I finished buttoning my jacket, and then said that he ought to know better, and that black comes in a hundred shades. With that, I brushed past him and left. I can think of many people who would have been terribly hurt by this comment. I can think of other moments in my life when such a comment would have hurt me, too.

In 1975, when I was eighteen, I took a summer job washing floors at Sunnybrook Hospital in Toronto. I was trying to rake in every possible cent because I was heading off to the University of British Columbia in the fall. Almost all of the workers—or certainly the floor-washers—at Sunnybrook were black immigrants from various Caribbean countries. They were almost all dark black, too. A handful of Greeks rounded out the crew. I was one of two lone summer students. The permanent workers were certainly friendly, but I knew that they didn't realize I was black.

One day at the hospital, in the change room, I told one of my fellow workers that my father was black. He didn't believe me. The next day, I brought in a photo. The man threw his hands in the air and shouted out to anyone within earshot, "This boy has a black father!" Half the crew came running. By the end of the shift, every single floor-washer at Sunnybrook Hospital knew that my father was black. Suddenly, they were all talking about it and inviting me to parties.

Notice that I said, "My father is black." I did not have the courage to say, "I am black." I knew that my fellow worker would have laughed me out of the room if I had tried that.

We blacks of light skin are used to the fact that we may, from time to time, be subjected to racism. Still, those of us who seek to identify with black people can feel insecure about the depth of our belonging. Will we be dissed? Challenged? Told outright that we don't belong?

It seems to me as certain as the setting sun that just as the occasional white person is going to try to hold you back because you're black, the occasional black person is going to diss you because you're not black enough. But why does the rejection hurt more when it comes from black people? I think it's because people with one black and one white parent move through a subconscious process that works like this: *I can't possibly be white. I am not white, although I have one white parent, will never really be viewed as white, and can't see myself as white, either. I can, however, be black, and that's the identity I'm choosing to claim.* Having relinquished (or been denied) one aspect of our racial identity, we feel insecure when our adoptive choice is rejected by the very people with whom we choose to identify.

But for the Interference with His Arrangement

Knowing that it featured an interracial relationship, I went to see the Hollywood flick *Save the Last Dance*. It features the actress Julia Stiles, who plays Sara, a white high school senior who moves into an all-black school in Chicago, and Sean Patrick Thomas, who plays Derek, a black high school senior who wants to become a doctor and is the only one in his peer group to show professional promise.

As is typical in movies, we get to sit in on the black experience—in this case, life among black students in an inner-city school—through the perspective of a white interloper. Ain't this always the way? We get it in *Dangerous Minds*, *Out of Africa*, *Music of the Heart*, *The Power of One*, *Losing Isaiah*, *Driving Miss Daisy*, and *The Green Mile*, to name a few.

At any rate, as Sara and Derek draw closer in *Save the Last Dance*, Derek's sister—who obviously is black—begins giving Sara a hard time for going out with a black guy and for snapping up one of the few who is not dead, drugged, or doing time. As Derek's sister vented her anger on Sara, I could hear a few people in the audience behind me clucking with disgust and irritation. I could just hear their thoughts: *What an idiot! What business is this of hers? Why shouldn't two people just be able to love each other?*

What struck me about the moviegoers' reaction was the ease with which they dismissed the black woman's anger. In real life, I often find this same peremptory dismissal of the frustration that some black women feel when they see black men taking white women as partners. Many white people write it off as racist and immature, and some black people diss it, too. But interracial dating is a troubling issue for some black women, and their negative reactions, when they arise, are very real. Rather than moving so quickly to invalidate this anger, I think we should try to understand what lies at its heart.

· · ·

As a boy, I heard and read about the humiliations, mutilations, and deaths that black men had faced over the centuries if they so much as let their eyeballs fall on a white woman. These deaths had come at the hands of white people, and it was a fact of life in the ugly pages of our history. But it was not until I was fifteen or so, and read *The Autobiography of Malcolm X* and *Soul on Ice* back to back, that I became aware that not every black person in the world would look with benevolence upon the union of my mother and my father.

Until he dropped his anti-white hatred after travelling in the Middle East and meeting Muslims of various races, Malcolm X preached that the white woman was the devil. *Soul on Ice* was even more disconcerting. In it, Eldridge Cleaver—who wrote the book in prison and acknowledged that he had raped both black and white women—described how one day a prison guard had torn down his poster of a white pin-up girl. Cleaver wrote, "The disturbing part of the whole incident was that a terrible feeling of guilt came over me as I realized that I had chosen the picture of the white girl over the available pictures of black girls . . . Was it true, did I really prefer white girls over black? The conclusion was clear and inescapable . . . I did . . . As a matter of course, a black growing up in America is indoctrinated with the white race's standard of beauty . . . It intensified my frustrations to know that I was indoctrinated to see the white woman as more beautiful and desirable than my own black woman."

This idea troubled me immensely. I wondered, for the first time in my life, about my father's motives in taking my mother, a white woman, as his partner. And I wondered about my mother's motives in taking my father, a black man, as her partner. Was I the product of a love that transcended racial indoctrination and self-hatred? Or had my parents come together for all the crass reasons pointed out by social critics like Cleaver: did she want the legendary sexual prowess of a black man, and did he hate all black women because they reminded him of the historic emasculation of the black male in America?

Over time, I came to believe again in the very genuine love that my parents have for each other. But I have never forgotten the anger and the accusation in *Soul on Ice*, and from time to time I still think about it. When I sat down to write this book, I decided to revisit this age-old, emotionally charged issue of black men loving white women. And I decided to start by looking at my own family and at myself.

To the best of my knowledge, none of the relatives on my mother's side of the family, with the exception of my mother herself, have taken black partners. But on my father's side of the family, plenty of interracial relationships must have taken place. His mother and many of her relatives were fair-skinned black folks, some of whom could occasionally pass for white.

My father says that he can't bring himself around to accepting the anger that some blacks display toward black–white unions because it falls completely outside the values with which he was raised. I believe that completely. He and his relatives grew up in a grossly racist country. His own paternal great-grandparents, Richard Hill and Demias Crew, remained enslaved until Richard purchased their freedom in 1859 from a Maryland slave owner. As my grandfather and great-grandfather acquired university educations and became ordained ministers of the African Methodist Episcopal Church, they moved into the middle classes and adopted integrationist values. They wanted their children to move among people of all races. They passed these values along to my father, who, understandably, has little patience now for people who chastise black men for chasing white women.

In my interview with him, he told the story of how in 1951, when he had just left the United States and begun graduate studies in Toronto, he took a white woman to a dance run by the Universal Negro Improvement Association (UNIA).

"I introduced her to a number of the black girls I knew. One of them said, 'Why did you bring her here?' and cussed me out. I told her that she was a racist. I said she ought to be ashamed of herself. I was a black man bringing a white girl to that dance, and she was affronted. That was the last time I brought any girl to the UNIA hall."

Ironically, my mother showed much more empathy for the anger of black women on this issue. "I've always felt very badly about the fact that disproportionately, black women were left out," she explained. "Because black men were marrying white women, and white men showed very little inclination to marry black women. I feel a great empathy. The white women in general are marrying, as they say, the best of the crop—the achievers in the black community. Those achievers are picking white women, and I feel badly about it. There's nothing I can do about it, because it's a societal phenomenon, but I do feel very badly for black women. In the Toronto hospitals, where Dad has been treated by all kinds of nurses, I have sensed, although it may have been my imagination, that many of the black nurses were not very friendly to me. I don't want people to stop mixing, but I wish there were white males mixing with black females."

. . .

Although my parents formed the only interracial couple of their generation in either of their families, there is a history of "involuntary mixing" in the family. One such story came to me by way of my father's sister, Jeanne Flateau, now eighty-two, who is one tough cookie. Jeanne graduated with a Bachelor of Science from the University of California at Berkeley in 1940, was a social worker and manager for the City of New York for twenty-eight years, and raised seven children in Brooklyn—every one of whom now has at least one university degree. Jeanne also has deep brown skin. There is not a nanosecond of doubt about this woman's race.

Jeanne sometimes says this of other people—particularly lippy children or grandchildren—but she, too, "has quite a mouth on her." She doesn't indulge fools or their foolishness. Once, when I was seventeen or so and had taken the bus to New York City to visit the Flateau family, Jeanne and I were getting off the subway at the Classon Avenue stop on the G line. We got out on the edge of Bedford-

Stuyvesant, and when we left the subway platform, I headed toward the wrong exit. "Git back over here, son," she said, grabbing my meatless Canadian biceps. "Hasn't anybody ever told you how to get out of a subway before? You don't walk up those steps. See how they hit that platform and then you have to head down another way, one you can't see from here? Somebody's sittin' right there waiting to remove your wallet, son, Canadian money and all. You take *those* steps. Over there. They go straight up to the street. You can see your way all the way up. Don't they have subways in Canada, or what?"

Jeanne is also known to have used her fists from time to time. Family legend has it that a few years after she got married to Sidney Flateau—a light-skinned Louisiana man of black, Cajun, and Indian origins—the newlyweds were visiting my grandparents in Washington, D.C. "Sidney said something to my grandmother that I considered to be disrespectful," Jeanne said, cackling with laughter as she recalled the incident, "so I told him to take off his glasses and I slapped him."

Decades later, when Jeanne was in ill health and, for a short while, disoriented, she found herself being checked out by an intern in a New York hospital. "Mrs. Flateau," asked the unfortunate young doctor, "are you suffering from any sort of psychiatric disorder?" "How dare you speak like that to me," she said, and delivered the second famous slap of her lifetime.

One of our classic family stories dates back to 1920, when Jeanne was one month old. Jeanne's grandmother, Marie Coakley, was a very light-skinned upper-crust black woman of the famed "black bourgeoisie." According to Jeanne, Marie "had dead-straight hair and looked white," but she married a black man and lived out her life in black communities. My understanding is that Marie, who was born in 1876, could pass for white but did so only occasionally.

In 1920, Marie dropped in on a white Catholic church in Philadelphia, met with the priest, and arranged without a hitch for her granddaughter, my aunt Jeanne, to be baptized there. A little later, Marie returned to the church to finalize matters, this time with her daughter and her son-in-law. They, of course, were all visibly black, and the priest was enraged. "When my mother and father showed up, the priest had a fit," Jeanne said. "He had assumed that I would be a white child, and he refused to baptize me."

Insulted, Marie Coakley took her baby granddaughter to a black Catholic church, also in Philadelphia, where she was finally baptized. This marked the beginning of my own grandmother's gradual disenchantment with the Catholic church (although Jeanne insists that the white Protestant churches of the day were just as racist). Ironically, my aunt remained in the church until 1985, when she finally moved over to the African Methodist Episcopal Church.

Another family legend explains how it came to be that Jeanne's grandmother, Marie Coakley, was so light-skinned that she could pass for white. The explanation for Marie's virtually white complexion? Jeanne acknowledges that one of her maternal ancestors was a white, Irish Catholic, and that the usual raping and plundering of her more distant slave ancestors had likely taken place.

"However, there was also involuntary mixing in the White House," Jeanne quips.

Family lore has it that Marie's mother, Maria Coakley, was employed as a maid or a seamstress in the White House in 1875. Ulysses S. Grant was the Republican president at the time, and Jeanne couldn't prevent herself from asserting that the man was "a notorious drunk." At any rate, Jeanne said that a white employee—nobody knows who—raped and impregnated Maria Coakley. "It would have done no good at all for a black employee of the White House to make any charges against any of the people," Jeanne said. "They wouldn't have believed her. Back then it was out of the question to even try to protest."

Maria Coakley remained in her home, and when she gave birth to baby Marie on February 21, 1876, the infant was raised as one of the children of her grandparents, Jenny and Gabriel Coakley. Her many "siblings" and her "parents" were all considerably darker in complexion.

My aunt Jeanne didn't learn of this story until she was twenty-one or so and living in Jersey City. Her grandmother Marie and her great-aunt Gertrude were visiting one day and launched into a fight. Marie said something insulting to Gertrude. Gertrude shot back that Marie was a bastard, and taunted her with the story of how she came to be conceived during a White House rape.

I asked Jeanne if she believes the story. "It is probably true," she answered. "Things like that happened all the time."

· · ·

In 1959, six years after my parents married and three years after I was born, a circuit court judge in Caroline County, Virginia—located within easy driving distance of my parents' wedding chapel—sentenced Mildred Jeter, a black woman, and Richard Loving, her white husband, to a year in jail for being married and therefore violating the state's ban on interracial marriages. (The couple had been married in the District of Columbia.)

The judge suspended the sentence on the condition that the Lovings leave the state and not return to Virginia together for twenty-five years. In his decision, he stated, "Almighty God created the races white, black, yellow, malay, and red, and he placed them on separate continents. And but for the interference with his arrangement there would be no cause for such marriages. The fact that he separated the races shows that he did not intend for the races to mix."

Mildred Jeter and Richard Loving (who couldn't have been more aptly named) appealed the verdict on the grounds that it violated the 14th Amendment to the U.S. Constitution, which states, "All persons born or naturalized in the United States and subject to the jurisdiction thereof, are citizens of the United States and of the State wherein they reside. No State shall make or enforce any law which shall abridge the privileges or immunities of citizens of the United States; nor shall any State deprive any person of life, liberty, or property, without due process of law; nor deny to any person within its jurisdiction the equal protection of the laws."

The couple lost in the first two appeals, including one to the Supreme Court of Appeals of Virginia. Eight years after the first ruling, however, the U.S. Supreme Court finally reversed the lower-court decisions and upheld the rights of the interracial couple.

Loads of American laws remained, of course, outlawing the union of blacks and whites. I own an amazing book entitled *States' Laws on Race and Color*. The 746-page volume, compiled in 1950 and published by the Woman's Division of Christian Service of the Methodist Church, is a straightforward compilation of every U.S. state law enforcing racial segregation that could be found by the author, a black American woman lawyer named Pauli Murray. So

lest we be too quick to condemn black women for express-
ing occasional anger at the sight of their brothers crossing
the colour line, let's remember that their reaction is but a
droplet of water in the hurricane of opposition that for centuries has rained down upon black men who even dreamed
of brushing their lips against white skin.

• • •

If I want to discuss the issue of the race-related choices in
partners that people make, I should acknowledge my own
choices, and those of some of my immediate family members.

I'll start with my father's three sisters. Jeanne's seven
children and Margaret's two children all married black
partners, although one of my cousins, upon remarrying,
took up with a Korean American. Doris's four grown children have each taken a white spouse.

My sister Karen married a white man in Germany,
divorced him, and while remaining in Berlin became
involved with a black Sudanese man, who is the father of my
niece Malaika. Karen and Malaika now live alone in Toronto.

My brother Dan has never to my knowledge been
involved with a black woman. In 1982, he married a white
woman, Bev Chapin. They remain together, have one son,
David, and live in Toronto.

I interviewed Dan for this book on December 13, 2000, in
Toronto, and he shared a revealing story dating back to
when he was seventeen years old and had reluctantly
accepted an invitation by a black girl to attend a Sadie
Hawkins dance. "I went to her high school, which was in
Scarborough, and I remember feeling very embarrassed
about being with a black girl, and very guilty about feeling
embarrassed, and feeling very cold toward her, as well as

being disappointed in myself. There was this huge, incredible conflict of guilt and shame, and strangeness. I remember that event being some sort of a peak, in terms of my conflicts about racial identity."

My father also tells a story that dates back to the late 1930s in Oakland, California, when he was enrolled in high school. "I was just beginning to go to dances with junior high school kids and high school kids, and my father pulled me over one day before I went to a dance and said, 'Son, I want to tell you something.' I said, 'Yes, Dad?' And he said, 'I want you to do something for yourself, and for me. Maybe at these dances, if you look carefully, you'll find a couple of girls who are sitting on the sidelines and will never get a dance, 'cause the guys go for all the light-skinned girls, the olive-coloured girls, and the black girls are stood up and never get an opportunity to dance because no one will ask them to dance. I want you to go, and before you start frolicking around, pick out the loneliest-looking, unhappiest-looking, blackest woman in the crowd, sitting on the sidelines, not being asked to dance. Go over and ask her to dance, and you dance with her.'

"I was a little shocked. I hadn't really thought this way. But I did start to think that way, and I did exactly what he said to do. And it sure was the truth, you know. I went to my next dance and there were two or three black women—sixteen-year-old-girls—sitting on the bench, not getting asked to dance, just sitting there all evening. I went over and danced with two of them. They seemed to appreciate it. I thought I did the right thing. And from then on, whenever I went to a public dance, I picked one of those black women to dance, the one who was the least handsome."

The approach seemed to me at the same time courteous and patronizing. Sensing, perhaps, the oddity of this description, my father noted that "wallflowers" who didn't get asked to dance could spend long evenings sitting alone. "Girls didn't dance with girls in those days. They were waiting for some young man to ask them to dance, and I did, and I reported back to my father that I did what he asked me to do."

Listening to family stories and stories shared by other interview subjects led me to start reviewing how race may have played into my own romantic choices in life.

With the exception of my first girlfriend, who was a Japanese Canadian, up to and including my seventeen-year marriage, I had always been involved with white women. Traditionally, I have been quick to point out that I simply didn't know any black women my age until my marriage ended in 1998. I have stated that there were no black girls in my neighbourhood, schools, track club, debating team, or social circles. I have said that I didn't meet one black woman at the University of British Columbia, where I studied in the mid-1970s, or at Université Laval, where I studied in the late 1970s. And those explanations were true. But they didn't acknowledge that I had grown up expecting and assuming that my romantic partners would be white. Living in an almost entirely white world certainly contributed to that expectation, as did the fact that I had a father who had chosen to spend his life with a white woman.

• • •

In 1996, a kerfuffle over a "wall of shame" erupted among students at Brown University in Rhode Island. Apparently, somebody had posted a list on campus—possibly in the privacy of one student's room—noting the black students who had dated white students.

The Brown *Daily Herald* ran an article on the issue, and quoted, among many others, Arhima Jacobs, a student living in Harambee House on campus (where the list appeared) and a co-chair of the university's Organization for United African Peoples. Jacobs set out to explain the anger that some black women feel when they see black men crossing the colour line. She mentioned that black men were "an endangered species," and that professional black men were even harder to find.

"There's a reason why black girls grow up thinking they're the ugliest things on the planet," Jacobs said. "I think it concerns us when we see the men in our community in their adulthood purposely turn away from African-American women when they choose a mate. It hurts to see that you are not wanted by your brother. I know if I was to have a black son, and he dated white women, it would seem to me to be a blatant rejection."

Markita Morris, another student at the time, had this to say to the *Herald*: "It makes me mad when people come down on any group of black women who have problems with interracial dating without knowing the history of it. Before you dismiss it, you need to know that a lot of people are seriously hurt by black men dating white women. Black women see this and it makes them upset. I think they have a right to be upset, but they need to choose the right way to express that hurt."

Patricia Hill Collins, a sociology professor in the Department of African-American Studies at the University of Cincinnati, describes the emotionally loaded history of black–white sexual relations in her excellent book *Black Feminist Thought: Knowledge, Consciousness and the Use of the Politics of Empowerment*. She quickly identifies the long history of sexual abuse of black women by white men as the fundamental tension underlying relationships between the two. "Such individual liaisons aggravate a collective sore spot because they recall historical master/slave relationships," she writes.

However, Collins notes, relationships between black men and white women remind black women that they have always been, and will continue to be, regarded as the least attractive or desirable group of women on the continent. Many black women end up living without a partner, acutely aware of their aloneness. Some keep on looking for a good black man. Others commit themselves to raising their children alone. Yet others devote themselves to professional careers, only to find that black men reject them because they are independent and white men turn away from them because they are black. "In this context," Collins writes, "heterosexual Black women become competitors, most searching for the elusive Black male, with many resenting the White women who naively claim them."

Collins zooms in on the culture of innocence that some white people reflect when they express astonishment at— and then summarily reject—the anger of black women in this regard. "In this context of what is perceived as widespread rejection by Black men, often in favour of White women, African-American women's relationships with Whites take on a certain intensity. On the one hand, antagonism can characterize relationships between Black and White women, especially those who appear blissfully unaware of the sexual politics that privileges White skin. Despite claims of shared sisterhood, heterosexual women remain competitors in a competition that many White women do not even know they have entered ... On the other hand, given the culpability of White men in creating and maintaining these sexual politics, Black women remain reluctant to love White men. Constrained by social norms that deem us unworthy of White men and norms of Black society that identify Black women who cross the color line as traitors to the race, many Black women remain alone."

• • •

When I began interviews for this book, I found that interracial dating was a hot topic. And I soon had almost as many opinions as I had interview subjects. Some of the women I interviewed spoke passionately in favour of the right of people to choose interracial relationships. One was Carol Alyward, of Halifax.

"Call me naive but . . . I've always believed that people should marry whomever the hell they want to marry. I think interracial relationships are normal." Carol said she understood but did not agree with complaints about black men choosing white women. "Love is irrational. Choosing a white partner isn't a rejection of black women." She also contested the common assumption that more black men than women form interracial relationships.

Carol pointed out that some black women say that instead of taking white women as partners, black men should help rebuild their own racial communities, long decimated by slavery and segregation. "These are ill-founded political beliefs being superimposed over very private decisions about personal relationships," she said, rejecting this "politicization of relationships."

Another interviewee who came down strongly in favour of freedom of choice was Jazz Miller, a writer and magazine editor. Jazz was born in Nassau in 1971 and moved with her white mother to Ottawa at the age of three. She bristled at the mention of opposition to interracial relationships—regardless of who was opposing them.

Jazz was raised by her mother and has never lived with her father, who resides in the United States. She argued that you should go after "whoever you're hot for." Jazz complained that some people believe if you really just want sex, "somehow it's so much dirtier if you're a black man with a white woman."

"I was born from that—a white woman with a dark man," she said. "I don't want to hear any more of this bunk about how black men shouldn't go out with white women. My mother had a right to do whatever she wanted to do. If that's a bad thing, where does that leave me?"

I asked Jazz if she could understand that some black women feel cut out of the picture when black men choose white partners. But she had an answer for that. "They should start looking at white men. There aren't that many men for any woman to draw upon. [The argument against interracial dating] doesn't really hold up when you look at it. There is absolutely nothing I can identify with. When we have white people saying this, we label them Nazis."

Interestingly, Jazz—herself a single mother of a ten-year-old black son—dated white men after her marriage ended, but now prefers black men or, at least, "men of colour." "If I were ever to have more children, my husband could not be white, because Calvin would feel left out."

· · ·

One of the most fascinating meetings I had in researching this book took place with someone who did not formally qualify for an interview, since she does not have one black and one white parent. Sandra Hardie, born in Jamaica in 1963, has two black parents, but much white ancestry thrown in the mix. Like so many black people in this country, Sandra knows the meaning of migration. She moved from Kingston, Jamaica, to Miami, Florida, at the age of fourteen, and later that same year was sent to live with her mother and stepfather in Brandon, Manitoba, arriving the day before Christmas. Sandra now lives in Richmond Hill, Ontario, works in the computer software industry, and is the single mother of a six-year-old daughter.

Sandra empathizes with black women who object to black–white unions, and shared some real insight into the phenomenon. "I do understand it. There's a perception that there are few available black men. I may be making an assumption, but I think that in our community, I see instances of women tending to be a little more economically advanced than men. I don't know if it's because of opportunity—in a racist society, women are given more opportunity because men are seen as more threatening. Traditionally, when black women were able to become nurses and teachers, the men were kept as porters. Today, women tend to be looking for men of the same economic standing as themselves. And I think that there's the perception that if there is a smaller pool of black men at this level, then they feel quite pissed off that white women are fishing in their waters. I think that's what it is.

"I personally don't feel the anger about interracial unions. But I can see that if you perceive that there are only a few men out there for you, you could be angry that you couldn't get your hands on one or two of them because a woman of another colour got them. What would be a prerequisite to that would be a lack of interest in dating a white man. You'd have to be interested in dating a black man only, to feel that there were fewer options open to you.

"But it seems to me that it is more common for black men to seek out white women than the reverse. I don't know why black men would be more inclined to go outside of the race than black women. I don't know if it's residual animosity with regard to slavery and the rapes of great-grandmothers, because it's not something that's been discussed a lot near me. I don't know what the hesitation is for black women.

"I have a friend who is living with a black woman, and he said to me, 'Before I marry her, I have to have me a white woman.' He's been raised in Jamaica, where whiteness is something to aspire to, and it's a jewel he's never touched—he wants to try this thing. On the part of the black man, it's this forbidden kind of thing that he gets to do. In the same vein, I know some white women who will date only black men, regardless of the content of their character. They want what they perceive to be a stud, a heavily endowed black man.

"Do you know the 'idiot seat,' right across from a bus driver, where an idiot sits and talks at the top of their lungs to the driver? Well, once I saw a white women in the idiot seat, in Winnipeg, in the early 1980s. It was a black bus driver, and she said to him, 'Is it really true, what they say?' Nudge, nudge, wink, wink. 'About black men?' He looked over and said, 'No, it's not true. Actually, most black men hang only two inches. That is, two inches off the ground.' I wanted to go up there and slap him off the bus."

Sandra then began to speak about a phenomenon she had dubbed "Rent-a-Dread," when white women travel to the Caribbean to cavort with black men. "The women I know who have done this would be considered unattractive by North American standards. They're white women who are quite large, and probably don't do much attracting of any colour here, based on the Barbie-doll image that we all want. One Winnipeg girl went to Jamaica three or four times a year for the purpose of sexual pleasure. Once she said to me, 'The blacker the better.' This isn't always true throughout the country, but dark-skinned people are generally in less-advantaged positions, so she liked the fact that men who were really economically disadvantaged would be even more willing partners. So she went and looked for men who were very dark and very poor, because then they would be even more grateful.

"Women like this don't necessarily make a direct payment, as in 'Thanks for the service, here's the money,' but they do leave gifts, money, and sometimes even the promise of sponsorship. There's that factor as well. And these men do this fifty-two weeks a year. You're as beautiful as the next girl who gets off the plane. It's a business.

"It doesn't offend me. But I think it's quite sad to know that a woman is so unattractive in her own home that she has to go looking for these things to make herself feel better. For the men, this is strictly economics. These men are usually married with children, or at least living with a woman. It's an ego thing as well, but it's mainly for financial opportunity. The need to feed is at the heart of it."

Although Sandra herself has dated interracially in the past and says she isn't troubled by the sight of a black man with a white woman on his arm, she has seen the anger at work.

"I saw it very clearly one evening. We were at a gathering of people in a home, and a dark-skinned single woman was sitting there, and in walked a very interesting-looking black man with a white woman on his arm. This man had a great career, and was interesting, educated, well versed on a lot of topics, so the conversation was going very well. And I suddenly noticed the black woman sitting there, using her eyes to throw darts at this man. She was very angry. And it didn't dawn on me at first what she could be angry about. I wondered if it was something we'd said that may have offended her.

"She was staring at this man and his woman, knitting her brows. You could tell she was very upset about them being there. I didn't have nice thoughts about her. She's not a woman that a black man *or* a white man would date. She's very harsh, with a caustic, vituperative tongue. I think she was just being hopeful that this man would look in her direction, had he not been in love with this white woman he was married to. There was no chance he would've been attracted to her even if he hadn't had this white woman. People did not get along with her very well."

Still, Sandra said she could understand the woman's frustration. "It's legitimate. I may not feel it or think it necessary, but there are women who do—and they feel it very deeply. And that again is very sad. To some degree, you have to feel that you are unlovable to have that reaction. If a black man is with a white woman just because she's white, then you don't want him. He's superficial, unworthy. So you have to have a feeling of self-worth to step over that and say, 'Please! Some trifling black man!' And see the Chinese man over there, or the white man over there, who might be a lot more deep in terms of his character and so on. It says something about black women when they have this gut reaction. You have to look at what's missing from you as well."

I asked Sandra what she thought of black women who insist they will never date outside the race.

"It is racist to say, 'I would never date a white man.' How can you say this? There's a billion people you've just eliminated with that statement, and you can't do that. You don't know people's characters individually, so to wipe them away like that is wrong. I basically think you shortchange yourself by pursuing that. I do think it's very sad when black peoples' gut reaction to seeing interracial relationships

is that of disgust. It is a very racist reaction. We limit ourselves when we do that.

"I have also on occasion heard black men say, 'I have to
check out that white woman, she's so beautiful,' and you
know that it's only because this woman is blond and white.
I find that irritating. I just don't like to see when my own
black men act stupid. It annoys me, but it's nothing that I
internalize personally."

Sandra felt the same way about white women who will
only date black men. "It comes down to rebellion, to seeking the exotic. A lot of the women who date black men just
because they're black have a great deal of insecurity. It's different, so it gives them a feeling of superiority over their
friends. They're doing something so forbidden. Rebellion
against family norm. But it has nothing to do with whether
this person is good or bad because invariably they choose
the worst of the lot. They choose black men that I wouldn't
even look at. I'm actually quite happy that they take them
off my hands. No more wasting my time!"

· · ·

Before I started writing this book, I felt an unexamined
impatience with the idea, common among some black
women, that "their" men should stick to black women.
Lots of men I know wouldn't hesitate to date a white
woman, or marry her, or have children with her. I certainly
never stopped to worry about it. I asked a few other men of
mixed race about their feelings on the subject. Ivan Gibbs
explained that his thinking has changed over time.

Ivan has had a rough life. He was raised singlehandedly
by his mother, a white woman, in Montreal, Quebec's Eastern Townships, Haiti, and Toronto. As a student at a
Toronto high school, he ended up using drugs, selling them,

and letting his anger get the better of him. He finally got kicked out of high school and was jailed for nearly two years for violent offences. Today, he has been out of jail for several years, has been working regularly in Montreal, is keeping fit in a gym, and is hoping to enter university and eventually become a sports journalist.

Although he dated black women exclusively for a time in his teens, Ivan said he doesn't care about race now, in terms of potential partners. "I am completely impartial—it doesn't matter to me what colour, race, creed, whatever. As long as you're hot, it's cool with me, but even that is changing now. I'm looking for something a little bit deeper . . .

"I want to have children because I think I'd be a good father. However, a lot of my friends have kids at a young age, and I see what kind of life they live. When I'm firmly established, with a roof over my head and a good woman who's going to be with me, then I will start trying to have children. I used to say before that it's got to be with a black woman, because I want my kid to come out dark so we can keep it going. My views on that have changed also. I don't care. Hey, my kid is my kid. I don't care who I have my child with, and I'll teach him or her the same thing.

"It would be hypocritical of me [to choose a partner based on race]. What happens if I'm in love with a white woman or an Asian woman, or whatever the case may be, and the topic of children comes up? What am I going to say, 'I can't. I'm sorry, it's got to be with a black woman'? No. It's crazy. Whoever I have it with is who I have it with and that's it. I'm not going to force myself to be with somebody because of their colour. That's ridiculous."

I asked Ivan what he thought about the frustration that some black women feel when they see black men taking white partners.

"I'm not going to pass judgement on them if they feel that way," he told me. "They feel raising their child that way is the best way, to have a child with a black man. [For me], the woman that I'm with, she's just as important as the child is to me, because I don't want custody battles, I don't want to see my child on the weekends only. I want my child to be with me all of the time and I want his mother with him all the time. That's it, it's a family. I've got to make sure that this woman is the woman for me [whatever her colour]."

· · ·

When I interviewed Cindy Henwood, who dates a black man, she raised the issue of his own dating preferences when it came to race. "He made it very clear that race would never be an issue for him, that he would date somebody no matter what colour they were, and he has. I've heard that from many black men—that race is not an issue or a problem if you love somebody. I think that it doesn't matter to them because they want to date white women. That is what is attractive, that's the way it's been since they were growing up, when they were boys. They wanted the girls with the long hair, with the light skin, white or whatever."

Cindy was one interview subject who acknowledged that she has definitely felt hostility when seeing black men with white women. "Here we go again" is how she describes her thought process, at least occasionally, in such circumstances. The first time she saw the man who would later become her boyfriend, she was on the dance floor at a wedding party in Toronto. "I turned and I looked and he was doing some kind of crazy dance. Later, he said he was trying to get my attention . . . but all I saw was a black man and a white woman and I thought, 'Here we go again.'

"Growing up on the prairies, I saw a lot of black men

who would only date white women. Again, the whole perception is that the standard of beauty is white, the standard
of beauty is long hair, blond hair. All of these things I knew
I could never have, although I have to say that as a light-
skinned black woman, my experiences are very different
from someone who is dark skinned, and I probably have
received more attention than a darker-skinned woman
might from black men.

"Then there's the stereotype that black men are dating
white women regardless of what they look like or how
intelligent they are, just for the fact that they are white. I've
heard black girls talking about this all the time. I've heard a
lot of black women talk about the fact that black men will
date white women as a status thing, especially if they begin
to do better financially. It's a showpiece to say, 'Not only
have I moved up in the world, but I have a white woman on
my arm.' Then there's always the contrast that is made
between black women and white women. Black women are
said to be more aggressive and hostile. They say whatever's
on their mind, they have no couth, no tact. White women
are said to be more feminine.

"I've heard a lot of black men say this, especially in
Saskatchewan. What you see a lot of is American black men
coming up, the football players. There are not a lot of black
people in Saskatoon, but during the summer for a certain
time, there are a lot of black men because of the baseball
players and the football players who come up from the
States. So in the restaurants, in the clubs, you'll see all these
black men with white women who are star-struck and
wanting to date professional athletes. I think that's where a
lot of the stereotypes come from, and I hear black women
complaining about it every summer. It's like, 'Oh, here we
go again.' You see a lot of star-struck women and these

black men are taking advantage of them and using them and having them do their laundry or drive them all over town, and these girls will do it just because they want to be dating a professional athlete, and black men are cool."

Cindy noted, however, that she has rarely seen black women chase white men in the same way.

"I don't think that black women want to date white men. I think that a lot of black women prefer to be with black men. I find that I am attracted to black men. I feel like I'm stating all these stereotypes, and I know that they are stereotypes, but there's just that whole comfort level thing, that familiarity. The fact that I can refer to a song or a TV show or I can use certain slang words, and that person will intuitively know where I'm coming from because he's been through the exact same thing. That is not to say that all black people have the same experiences, because obviously that's not true. But I will always argue that there are tangible things that you can put your finger on and say this, this, this, and this, and we've all experienced these things."

Cindy said that part of her desire to be with a black man stemmed from a conscious wish to live within and contribute to a black community. "This is something that I've thought about recently. I think for me it's important that when I have children, I want them not to have the same sort of ambiguity in terms of physical appearance. I want them at least to not have to be questioned. I'm not necessarily saying that I want them to look black, but I want them to have that sense of belonging that I never had or that I had taken away from me many times. I enjoy and am drawn to all the elements of black culture, and I want my children to fully experience and enjoy and be part of it. I don't think a lot of black men think about that."

. . .

On the issue of relationships between black men and white women, I wanted to hear directly from some black women. One of them was Elaine Brooks, who was born in 1961, and who lives in Scarborough.

"It's a visceral response," Elaine said. "It just sets me in this self-esteem whirlwind, or lack of self-esteem. I was nine when my mother and father [who were both black] separated, and my father hooked up with Wendy [not her real name], a white woman, right away. The first male relationship a girl has is with her father. So when my father went with a white woman, it was like he was not validating who I was as a black woman. It felt like my mother wasn't good enough, I wasn't good enough, my family wasn't good enough. Whether this was something real, or whether it's a childhood memory of loss and pain, is another matter. But that is one thing I do remember."

Elaine said that she could only guess about her father's motivation in choosing a white wife. But she did note that her father had been moving up in his career, at the time, and that Wendy, who was much younger and white, might have been seen by some as a "trophy wife."

"As an individual, everybody should make their own choice, right? I look at my brother [happily married to a white woman]—he made a perfect choice. I look at my sister and her husband—mind you, that was more of an enigma, black woman with a white man. But it's also part of that whole discussion about cutting down who's left to date, as far as black women are concerned. That's part of it, but it's not really what hurts me.

"I feel like black men are saying that black women aren't good enough for them anymore. Or aren't good enough, period. Or this is better than what they've known before. Or this is who you should be emulating."

Elaine acknowledged that she didn't have the same freedom to move across racial boundaries as, say, an average black man might have, and that this has affected her dating choices. "I learned that lesson early. So early, in fact, that I kind of discounted it. As soon as I was beginning university, maybe twenty years ago, I discounted dating white men." Her clear impression is that more black men date white women than the other way around.

"I refer to my sister [a black woman married to a white man] as the 'enigma' in her relationship. She knows exactly what I'm talking about. She laughs because Bob thought she was an African transfer student or something when he first met her. But Bob's an enigma as well. He came up through a family that adopted two black children in 1960 and 1964."

I mentioned to Elaine that some people can't understand the anger that some black women feel about interracial dating.

"I think it's 'cause of how some black women behave. When they express it, some of them express it in a really sharp, churlish way. They may say something nasty. I've been in places where I've seen women . . . they don't even *know* the person, and they're cussing them out, or they're making some kind of really rude comments. So they're making it a situation, they're just going emotionally with it. They're sucking their teeth, rolling their eyes, and they don't even know these people at all.

"A lot of it does resonate for black women in terms of being dissed, or not being respected by the black man. [It's the feeling] that she's not good enough. That we'd better add some more weave 'cause our tresses aren't long enough. It hits a lot of different places."

• • •

When I interviewed my sister, this topic highlighted one of our main differences. Before writing this book, I hadn't given much thought to race in the context of my romantic relationships. But Karen had. She imagined romantic relationships, and having a child, as opportunities to affirm her own blackness. And that I never did. I married a white woman and had three children and never gave any thought to whether they were or weren't contributing to my own sense of racial identity.

When my sister moved to Berlin, she ended up marrying a white German man and living with him for many years. When their marriage broke up in the mid-1980s, Karen remained in Germany but began to hang out at a Sudanese café and to associate much more with Africans who had moved abroad. Eventually, she became involved with a Sudanese man and became pregnant by him. The relationship with her Sudanese lover didn't get off the ground, however, and Karen moved back to Canada, with Malaika in her womb, in 1989.

"It was very clear that I wanted this child, and that I was glad that this child was going to be black. I was glad that this child was going to be blacker than I am, that she would be recognizably black to the outside non-black world. I felt that she would therefore—to a certain degree—somehow have it easier. I felt it was so hard [when I was young]. People would always ask me, 'My God, what the hell are you?' I thought with Malaika that probably wouldn't be the case."

Like a number of the mixed-race women I interviewed (but unlike virtually all of the mixed-race men), Karen expressed a real hesitancy about becoming involved with someone white.

"There are plenty of interesting white guys out there—I'm not saying it would never happen. I don't believe in saying you shouldn't be involved with people outside of your race. I think people should be involved with whomever they want to be involved with. I can only say that for myself, right now, there is a desire to find somebody who is non-white. I don't know if I can find white men who ever really understand fully the importance of race in my life. I guess I am more interested in men of colour. They could be South Asian, they could be Asian or Native, or they could be black. But somehow I feel that all those people will have some understanding of the problem or problems that I go through, that I face. So I wouldn't say that I would never consider it, but I feel like I've sort of 'been there, done that.' I think for a long time when Malaika was very young, I really wanted to find somebody who was black. I was thinking that I owed it to her. I felt scared at the beginning. When I first came back, I was scared about raising this child on my own. Was I going to be able to do justice to her? She was going to be even blacker than I am, and I really wanted that. But I was scared about whether I was really going to be able to do for her what I felt she needed. Was I strong enough, was I going to have it in me? Was I going to be able to get involved in the black community?"

Something else surprised me in the interview with Karen. It turned out that she had always been impressed by my involvement in the black community, and by my facial traits, which were more visibly "black" than hers. I, on the other hand, had always felt that my younger sister was more connected with the black community than I was, and had sometimes wished that I looked a little darker—like her. When I look back on how we saw each other's connections to the black community, I can understand why we both tended to admire each other's involvement—our connections were different. Karen's were social: friends, neighbours, and people to go drinking and dancing with. Mine were usually through volunteerism or my work as a writer. We each saw the other having community links that we lacked—and wanted.

Near the end of the interview, I asked if Karen ever felt angry when she saw black men with white women.

"I don't feel angry," she replied, "but I do feel frustration sometimes, because you think, 'Here we go again,' and you wonder, you know? Is it a genuine sort of thing, or are they parading a piece on their arm?"

I asked if she felt the same way about the white women. Were they also parading a piece on their arm?

"Yeah, sure. I feel very strongly about that. I knew white women who said they were going to Jamaica to find themselves a black stud and have themselves some great sex. It's the sexualization and exoticization of black men as sex objects only. They are good for sex. It's funny, because I don't feel that way if I see a black man and an Asian woman, or a black man and a South Asian woman. And you don't see that very much, so I always sort of react to that like, 'That's nice!' . . . [But with white women], I feel that they are going after something that is just a sexual relationship. Is that what it is all about? They are going after somebody who looks great, performs great, looks good on [her], looks cool. In Germany, I found a lot of women wanted to have children, black children or brown, because they thought they were cute. It was like the German women were looking for pieces of candy, to show off their children as fluffy little lollipops. Colourful things that people will ooh and aah over when they are young, and as soon as they grow up, they don't ooh and aah any more. The children are then treated in a racist manner, have to deal with all kinds of problems. The same people who were oohing and aahing have changed their tunes and are now talking about vandalism and black kids. Black babies are cute. Black teenagers aren't.

"Brown babies are even cuter because they are diluting the pool somehow and the nose isn't as thick, the lips aren't as thick . . . I've had people tell me that mixed-race children are the most beautiful children. That puts me in a place I don't want to be in. I don't want to feel more beautiful than someone else because I'm half black and half white and better, therefore, because I'm not as black."

. . .

I asked Sara, the anonymous interviewee from London, Ontario, if she had ever found herself reacting negatively to the sight of a black man with a white woman.

"Oh, yeah . . . I think that's why I had to date Peter [a white man, and not his real name], so I wouldn't be so judgemental in that arena. This is my bias. I don't think parents understand the complexities involved in being of mixed race. I don't think our parents sat down and thought about it.

"I took the right path. I did not want children from a white man. I made sure of that. I didn't want to create the confusion that I felt most of my life. I didn't want to reproduce that, you know? . . . I sat across the dinner table from my black dad, who had this thing for calling us mulatto—that just stopped, about three years ago—and my father's a black man from black parents and a black community. His experience will never be mine, and mine will never be his. So my dad could never define who I was. My dad thought, and I think in a well-intentioned way, that being of mixed race was maybe just a little bit better than being black.

"A woman at work has a sister married to a black guy and they have kids. Some kid had called her daughter a nigger.

The mother was upset—the mother's white—and the dad said, 'Oh, she'll have to get used to it.' The woman I work with was saying, 'My sister was uncomfortable with that reaction, but what could she say? What did she know? He knew better than she did.' And I said, 'Your brother-in-law might be right in that she has to grow thick skin. But I think what black parents of mixed-race kids don't understand is that their black experience is not going to be the same as that of their mixed-race kid.' So I'm not sure that would be an approach I'd take—I wouldn't say, 'Grow thick skin.' I'd have a discussion, talk about feelings, all that other jazz. But that kid is not gonna be a black kid, she's not gonna be a white kid. She's a mixed-race kid, and there's a difference.

"When I dated a white male, I fell in love with him, and it was very hard for me, and we talked a lot before I really got involved with him because it was hugely uncomfortable. I read what little there was to read on mixed-race couples, and it wasn't answering my questions. It was all this happy, touchy-feely talk, which I felt was bullshit."

When I asked Sara to explain her discomfort with dating a white partner, she was unequivocal. "White men raped black women for many years. Raped my grandmothers. My grandmothers were raped by white men, so how could I choose to lie with a white man when they'd wreaked so much havoc on women I knew?"

Sara's relationship with Peter's family didn't do much to alleviate her discomfort. "I met his mum on different occasions, and she was offensive and rude to me. So then we just spent time with his dad and his dad's family once we started dating. So then that upset Mummy, and Mummy started coming around, trying to make deals like 'Well, I'll be nice to her, I'll accept her. Come over and I'll take her to lunch.' I wouldn't concede. How many times do you stick your hand in the fire before you figure out that it burns? So I just wouldn't. My family accepted him with open arms, so he did whatever with my family and it was no big deal—talked to them on the phone, did all sorts of things with them—and it didn't always involve me. They genuinely like each other. But his family was different. I don't think it's ideal for me to be with a white person. It doesn't mean that I can't, or wouldn't, but I don't think it's ideal.

"I knew as far back as I can remember that I would never have kids with a white man. I knew that when I was ten years old. I could probably dig out old diaries. I didn't want mixed-race kids. I didn't want them to feel what I'd felt. It was just a painful experience that I would not want to repeat."

I asked Sara if her experiences dating a white person in some way took the steam out of the feelings she might have felt earlier about black men and white women.

"Yeah, sure. I was there myself, and I could appreciate falling in love with a person and then having to deal with the reality of race. Now, when I see mixed couples, I just think, wow. Hard work. It's hard work being in a relationship, and when you start adding layers to that, it's even more difficult. So yeah, I don't think it's ideal for me. I'm grateful I had the time that I had with Peter. He was a lot of fun, [and] he was good to me and my kids."

• • •

My thinking on interracial dating changed considerably as a result of the interviews I conducted, the books I read, and the self-examination I put myself through. I know what my own preferences are. If I meet someone I love and who loves me, I'll throw myself onto that runaway train, and I won't be stopping to worry about that person's ancestry. If we work together, then so be it. All else will fall into place. Is that naive? Maybe. Is my sense of love misplaced? It may seem so to some people, but I don't care.

However, I do respect the decisions that other individuals make. Most white people in this country take up with white partners. Do we run around all day asking ourselves what their hang-ups are with regard to race? No, sir. For the most part, we shrug our shoulders, accept that two people have formed a couple, and get on with our own lives. Some white people prefer whites. Some prefer Asians. Some prefer blacks. Some may prefer quadroons or octoroons. I don't really have the desire or the energy to question their decisions. I say, let them make love, and let them be.

I feel the same way, of course, about black people, and about all the other sorts of people I have not discussed much in this book: gays, lesbians, and people of every ancestry on the planet. I've got better things to do than devise a moral code that dictates whom they should or shouldn't be loving. There are millions of us out there, folks. Let's hope there will be room for all of us to make our own choices.

Some people have a romanticized notion that there is one perfect partner waiting for them in the world. I don't believe this. For every one of us, there are probably many people we could love intimately, and who could love us. However, the simple fact is that many of us remain alone, some of us by choice, and some of us by virtue of having been left out. Over and over again in my interviews with black women and women of mixed race, I heard that many of them have indeed felt left out—particularly because of the tendency of some black men to choose white partners.

In any loving relationship, you are supposed to respect your partner's feelings, and not to degrade or discount them. I want to have a loving attitude not just toward any intimate partner that I may have, but toward people in general. I want to be caring, accepting, thoughtful, and not too quick to apply moral judgements to the choices or feelings of other people. Although I respect the choices my parents made in crossing a huge racial divide and forming a life together, I also respect the hurt and anger and alienation that many black women feel in their lives, in their romantic relationships, and in their all-too-frequent solitude. These are the same women who—as grandmothers, sisters, aunts, neighbours, friends—are called upon to take care of black children when one of the biological parents—sometimes white, sometimes black—takes off. They are the same women who cook in churches, clean up at community events, and manage the twin challenges of pursuing careers and nurturing communities. And they truly bear the overwhelming majority of the work of transmitting culture, values, love, and self-respect to black children. So the next time you hear a black woman sucking her teeth when she sees a white woman in a black man's arms, think twice before you diss her.

No Negroes Here

In June 2000, an editor at the *Globe and Mail* asked me to write an opinion piece about a sensational custody battle in British Columbia. Theodore "Blue" Edwards, a black American millionaire who had formerly played basketball with the Vancouver Grizzlies, was fighting Kimberly Van de Perre, a white woman who lived in a basement apartment and was frequently unemployed, over the custody of their mixed-race son. I couldn't resist the offer, especially when I learned that the Vancouver media were up in arms over a decision by the B.C. Court of Appeal to award custody to the father, partly on the basis of race.

When I scratched beneath the lurid surface of the warring ex-lovers' story, I found the case fascinating and troubling. Apart from being a legal battle that I knew would generate debates about race and custody in households across Canada, it also raised issues of class, power, and gender. Theodore Edwards is university educated, a highly successful athlete, and rich by any standard. He is represented by one of Vancouver's most prestigious lawyers. Kimberly Van de Perre dropped out of high school, and prior to this custody fight, her only claim to fame was that she once won a beauty contest in Vancouver. She currently works part time as a hotel receptionist, and could be struggling for years to pay her legal bills.

Elijah Van de Perre is the boy in the middle. His parents have been in litigation since he was ten weeks old, and he turned four just days before his case landed in the laps of the nine white justices of the Supreme Court of Canada, to which the case was appealed in June 2001. I found myself hoping that Elijah's custody would be settled as quickly as possible, so that he wouldn't have to continue the absurd arrangement of flying between his mother's apartment in Vancouver and his father's home in Charlotte, North Carolina, every three weeks. As well, I wanted the lawyers, judges, and media involved in the case to examine the underlying racial issues. It doesn't appear that either wish will come true. At the time of writing, the Supreme Court has reserved judgment, and the case has already spent four years crawling through three courts. And Canadians, being Canadians, have once more proven our mastery of the art of burying our heads in the sand—insisting that race doesn't matter in this country.

· · ·

I told my father that I would be travelling to Ottawa to sit in on the Supreme Court hearing, and mentioned that in written arguments submitted in advance to the court, lawyers representing Theodore Edwards and Kimberly Van de Perre had skirted any serious discussion of racial issues. I wondered if he would comment on a certain irony at play. After all, it is largely because of Theodore Edwards, a black American who only lived three years in this country, that Canadians were being asked to think about race. Dad just shook his head sadly and said, "Some things never change."

I asked what he meant. "Read my thesis again," he said heavily. He was talking about *Negroes in Toronto: A Sociological Study of a Minority Group*—his University of Toronto doctoral dissertation, which he finished in 1960.

I went home and flipped open the 410-page brick, which was groundbreaking at the time. Coming as he did from living his first thirty years in the United States, where racism was discussed openly, he noted in the thesis his surprise at how Canadians not only avoided the issue, but had difficulty bringing themselves to even pronounce the word "Negro," which was in vogue at the time. Poor Dad. He had just finished serving several years in the segregated U.S. Army. Such was his disgust for racism entrenched in every facet of American life that he chose to leave, forever, his own birthplace—the country of his parents, sisters, and friends. But, once he crossed the forty-ninth parallel, Dad found that many Canadians wouldn't talk about racial issues. He was stymied, for example, as he tried to interview and give out questionnaires to black and to white Canadians.

"In the course of interviews," Dad wrote in the thesis, "many people ... preferred not to be called Negro or coloured. A railroad porter who, with his family, had lived in Toronto for thirteen years, said: 'I know a lot of light skinned Jamaicans who live in this area, but they don't consider themselves coloured.'. . . If many people of Negroid ancestry are confused, or refuse to accept the designation Negro, the problem is equally prevalent among whites. Questionnaires returned from churches, regarding the number of Negro members, indicate that many ministers were hesitant in describing parishioners of Negroid ancestry. 'We have about half-a-dozen West Indians in our parish but they are, I understand, not classed as Negroes,' wrote one rector. Another clergyman, replying that no Negroes were members of his church, added that there were, however, "two families of dark-skinned Bermudans [*sic*]."

What strikes me about my father's experiences more than forty years ago in Toronto, and when considering how Canadians have avoided talking about race in the custody case involving Elijah Van de Perre, is that we can't resolve problems that remain unacknowledged.

Canadians don't like to talk about racism. It offends us. We like to think of ourselves as Boy Scouts and Girl Guides, as protectors of international human rights and peacekeepers. We don't like hearing that slavery existed right here in Canada until 1834. We don't like being told that some slave-owning legislators prevented John Graves Simcoe, Upper Canada's first lieutenant-governor, from passing a law to abolish slavery in 1793. (In the end, Simcoe had to compromise, and the legislature passed a law that barred any more slaves from being imported into the province and set existing slaves free at the age of twenty-five.) We don't like being told that at about the same time in Nova Scotia, 1,200 black United Empire Loyalists became so disgruntled with broken promises and bad treatment that they left Halifax and sailed to Sierra Leone in Africa—at a time when the transatlantic slave trade was still booming. We don't appreciate it when historians such as James Walker at the University of Waterloo observe that our very own Supreme Court has made some truly frightful rulings in the past, such as backing in 1914 a Saskatchewan law that barred "Chinamen" from hiring white women and upholding in 1939 the right of a Montreal bar to exclude a black patron.

Although we blandly embrace federal multiculturalism policies and are more than happy to watch black folks shake their backsides during Caribana, we sure don't want to hear that until the 1960s, the Canadian government deftly prevented thousands upon thousands of blacks and Asians from applying to come to Canada. One sleight of hand that the Canadian government employed was to claim absurdly that blacks in countries such as Barbados and Jamaica weren't truly subjects of the Commonwealth and therefore couldn't benefit from immigration privileges extended to all (read "white") Commonwealth citizens.

Another trick, of course, was to pretend that it was for their own good that we were keeping blacks out of Canada. On May 10, 1951, for example, Walter Harris, then federal Minister of Citizenship and Immigration, wrote to York South MP J.W. Noseworthy, who was trying to help one of his West Indian constituents bring his granddaughter, Miss Una Jessamy Braithwaite, to Canada. I found the letter reproduced in my father's thesis. Here is the most revealing section of the letter:

"It is quite evident ... that Miss Braithwaite does not qualify for admission under present regulations and in the circumstances no encouragement can be offered ... In the light of experience it would be unrealistic to say that immigrants who have spent the greater part of their lives in tropical or sub-tropical countries become readily adapted to the Canadian mode of life which, to no small extent, is determined by climactic [sic] conditions. It is a matter of record that the natives of such countries are more apt to break down in health than immigrants from countries where the climate is more akin to that of Canada. It is equally true that, generally speaking, persons from tropical or sub-tropical countries find it more difficult to succeed in the highly competitive Canadian economy. It would be contrary to fact, however, to infer from this that colored immigrants are debarred from Canada. As in the past, favourable consideration is given in cases where the exceptional qualifications of the applicant offer reasonable assurance that he will find a satisfactory level in [the] Canadian community or where refusal would constitute extreme hardship on humanitarian grounds. This policy is inspired by a very sincere concern for the welfare of those who wish to share our way of life as well as by a justifiable sense of self interest."

Fine, some might say, *but that's old hat. That was forty or more years ago.* However, ample evidence exists in Canada that blacks are still punished for being black. Some teachers underestimate and discourage black students. Some police officers are more likely to shoot suspected criminals who are black. Some landlords and employers still find politely expressed Canadian ways to exclude potential tenants and employees because they are black. Blacks continue to turn up in the court system and in jails in a disproportionately high number. And if a black in Canada who is convicted of a serious crime is found to have been born in Jamaica, say, and not to have citizenship here—well, he may well be deported, even if he has lived here most of his life. It is well-nigh impossible to be a conscious and thinking black person—or a mixed-race person with some African heritage—and to not be aware that from time to time, and sometimes a great deal of the time, black people are watched and feared and kept at a distance by other Canadians. In this country, racism is like a fleet-footed bedbug that runs for cover under a sweet-smelling duvet stuffed with politeness and tolerance for multiculturalism.

I have not mentioned these blights on our past to castigate Canadians. On the whole, I don't think finger-pointing works. The best way to deal with problems is to focus on solutions—but first you have to name the problem. Elijah Van de Perre is the son of a black man and a white woman. For better or for worse, he will often be seen in Canada and the United States as a black person. That exposes him to a certain degree of risk. Few people today would disagree that girls have traditionally been discouraged from studying math and science in school, and that they can benefit from special encouragement in these areas in order to open up their opportunities in life. So what is the big deal in simply acknowledging that many black people will face challenges that arise as a result of their race? In Canada, custody fights are supposed to be decided on the basis of the child's best interests. To my way of thinking, Elijah's best interests must include the encouragement of his racial self-esteem and confidence. Let's turn now to his case, and see how it has been handled thus far by the courts and the media.

. . .

On the hot, sunny day that this custody fight came to Ottawa, reporters, photographers, and television crews camped out early in the morning on the steps leading up to the magisterial Supreme Court of Canada. Camera crews filmed any person who walked by, just in case the footage could be used later on the evening news. Kimberly Van de Perre and Theodore Edwards both showed up, and their faces—white woman, black man—appeared in large colour photographs the next day on the front page of the *National Post*. This comes as no surprise. In North America, we've had a thirst for news about nocturnal carousing between black men and white women ever since African men were brought here in chains and made to stand and toil half naked in the sun.

Warnings notwithstanding, we all know what kind of trouble black men and white women like to get into. Over the four hundred-odd years since black men were so courteously invited to live in North America, we have done our

best to keep them from—well, you know what it is we
don't want them doing. (It was okay for white slave owners
to rape black women and to enslave their own children, but
we won't discuss that today.) Let's see here, we've tried
lynching, torture, anti-miscegenation laws, segregation, and
public ridicule. We've also tried good old-fashioned discrimination, such as the type my parents faced when they
moved from the U.S. to Toronto in the 1950s and couldn't
rent an apartment together. But the more that people kick
and scream about the carryings-on between black men and
white women, the more inclined they are to do whatever
they please. And why shouldn't they? Here on the sidelines, I'm clapping for them. Clapping in principle, at least.
In practice, however, the loving between Theodore
Edwards and Kimberly Van de Perre turned sour after she
got pregnant and had their baby.

Their story began in 1995, when Edwards moved to
British Columbia to play with the Vancouver Grizzlies.
Edwards, who was living with his black wife and their twin
daughters, soon began an extramarital sexual relationship
with Van de Perre. Edwards and Van de Perre were both
described in court documents as habitués of the NBA-
groupie scene. He was said to go trolling in nightclubs, and
she was said to nibble. As a result of an affair that lasted for
some eighteen months, Ms. Van de Perre became pregnant
and, in 1997, had a son named Elijah

After parting ways, Van de Perre and Edwards each spent
great amounts of energy and money in court, accusing the
other of sexual promiscuity. For example, the factum submitted by Van de Perre's lawyers to the Supreme Court of
Canada said, "Mr. Edwards fully participated in the NBA
'groupie' scene, frequenting bars where young, star-struck
women made themselves available to professional sports

stars. He had previously been caught by his wife in two extra-marital affairs."

Edwards's lawyers responded with even nastier accusations in their own factum to Canada's highest court: "The appellant [Kimberly Van de Perre] is a twenty-four-year-old [actually, she was twenty-seven when the case went to the Supreme Court of Canada] single woman who dropped out of high school, worked sporadically at various jobs and was fired from several. She collected Social Assistance and Employment Insurance while not declaring the considerable amount of money the Respondent [Theodore Edwards] gave her. The Appellant has a long history of partying, promiscuity, and sexual pursuit of NBA players, other athletes and celebrities. She admitted lying and misleading under oath. At trial, she lied about her times and trips away from Elijah, who she left Elijah with, her many sexual partners, and the extent to which she put her social life before Elijah's interests."

At the first trial at the British Columbia Supreme Court, which stretched over twenty-six days in 1998 and 1999, Van de Perre's attack proved more effective. In awarding custody to Van de Perre, Justice J. Warren wrote, "In view of the father's extra-marital affairs, it was likely that he and his wife would separate." Interestingly, Justice Warren reached this conclusion even though Edwards and his wife, Valerie, had testified that their marriage remained solid. While on the witness stand, Valerie Edwards was asked "how many more affairs" she was willing to accept before she would "call it quits." In response, Valerie Edwards said, "I know all marriages have trials and tribulations and problems, and I am willing to stand by my husband, as long as he is still a loving man, a good father, and he is responsive to the family, and he puts the family focus first, I'm willing to stand by him as long as it takes, sir, until we're gray . . . I'm sure my mother had problems ... but she did not walk away. That's not our heritage, we're strong, black women. We don't run."

Let me interject briefly and say that I did sigh heavily upon first hearing of Valerie Edwards's quote. Strong black women don't run from what? Unhappy marriages? Husbands who have numerous affairs? I don't judge Kimberly Van de Perre or Theodore Edwards for having had their fun, but I did find it tiresome to see them slinging accusations of sexual promiscuity in court. As they say, it takes two to tango. Valerie Edwards, however, took the cake with her comment about strong black women. I bristled at the suggestion that, somehow, the ideal strong black woman was supposed to sit back and take it. It seemed to me to project the very stereotype that my parents always taught me to combat. Strong black women don't run? Why shouldn't they? If a marriage deteriorates to the point that the wife—who is, let's say, a strong black woman—needs to jump out of the starting blocks, all I have to say is, "Go girl. Go now. You've got a right to a life, whether you're strong or weak, nimble or klutzy, black, white, or any mixture thereof."

The issue of Elijah's racial identity was barely discussed in the B.C. Supreme Court trial. Lawyers on both sides largely avoided the issue, although Valerie Edwards was asked in cross-examination whether she agreed that Elijah's heritage was a complicating issue between the two biological parents. Ms. Edwards replied that Kimberly Van de Perre "couldn't teach him what it's going to be like to be black, and how he is going to be seen in the world as black, so no, she couldn't teach him that. And reading books won't help." She continued, "All I am saying is that [Elijah] should have an idea where he comes from, his background, his heritage; he should have that. He should have that fundamental. And I'm not sure if he's going to get that with [Kimberly Van de Perre]."

These arguments did not sway Justice J. Warren. In his decision, he wrote, "There is some evidence before me of the needs of the child to be exposed to his heritage and culture as the son of an African American, but there is also the need of the child to be exposed to the heritage and culture as the son of a Caucasian Canadian. There is, of course, the overarching need for the child to be secure in a stable and loving environment. By all accounts, [Kimberly Van de Perre] has provided such an environment since his birth. Of course, she has endured a very difficult pregnancy and the difficult time thereafter as a single parent caught up in the throes of a very hotly contested lawsuit. In my view, she has prevailed rather well given these circumstances."

One year later, the B.C. Court of Appeal overturned the first judicial decision. In writing a unanimous decision awarding custody to the father, Madam Justice Mary Newbury observed, "With respect, I'm not sure there is a 'Caucasian Canadian' culture." She criticized the lower court's "seemingly one-sided approach" that she said focused on Edwards's adulterous relationships while "failing to mention the negative aspects of the mother's character."

Madam Justice Newbury then went on to make a few comments about race that inflamed public opinion in British Columbia and fuelled even more media coverage. To begin with, Madam Justice Newbury criticized the lower court judge for giving "no consideration to issues of race and inter-racial problems as they relate to [Elijah Van de Perre], who is the product of a Caucasian mother and an Afro-American father. As much as one might wish it were otherwise, the existence of inter-racial problems in Canadian (and indeed North American) society cannot be ignored—as the Supreme Court of Canada has recently recognized in other contexts."

Near the end of her seventeen-page decision, Madam Justice Newbury wrote, "Finally, there are the matters of [Elijah's] race, or ethnicity, and the possibility of racial difficulties he may encounter in either family environment. These issues are . . . clearly relevant to the . . . best interests of the child, in particular to his health and emotional well-being."

The judge concurred with an observation made by Emily Carasco, a University of Windsor family law professor, who wrote in a 1999 edition of the *Canadian Journal of Family Law* that a child's well-being and future in our society are "inextricably linked" to the colour of his or her skin. Madam Justice Newbury proceeded to quote from Carasco's article, entitled "Race and Child Custody in Canada: Its Relevance and Role": "If a child's identity is influenced by its racial background . . . and categorization of the child by skin colour plays a significant role in influencing the child's future—then 'race' surely matters in a child's life. It is not a detachable factor that can be added on or ignored at will. 'Colour blindness' in these situations is not helpful to the child as it ignores or denies the political and social significance of 'race' and therefore ignores or denies the realities of that child's life."

Madam Justice Newbury's conclusion set off a storm of protest among those in the country who objected to the insertion of race into this custody battle. "If it is correct that [Elijah] will be seen by the world at large as 'being black,' it would obviously be in his interests to live with a parent or family who can nurture his identity as a person of colour and who can appreciate and understand the day-to-day realities that black people face in North American society—including discrimination and racism in various forms," she wrote. "It would certainly be naive to assume that [Elijah] would not encounter problems of racial prejudice at some point in his life in this country. The Supreme Court of Canada has found that there is 'systemic discrimination against black and aboriginal people' in Canada . . . This fact makes it impossible to accept the argument made by Mr. [Steven] Mansfield [Kimberly Van de Perre's lawyer] that there is no racism in Canada.

"It would also be naive to think that [Elijah] would not encounter racial prejudice growing up in the southern United States, where Mr. and Mrs. [Edwards] plan to settle in the long term. However, it seems to me likely that being raised in an Afro-American family in a part of the world where the black population is proportionately greater than it is here would to some extent be less difficult than it would be in Canada. [Elijah] would in this event have a greater chance of achieving a sense of cultural belonging and identity and would in his father have [a] strong role model who has succeeded in the world of professional sports.

"Canadian courts have adverted to the interrelated factors of culture, ethnicity and race in the context of child custody, although with little analytical rigour. . . . I do not propose to try to introduce greater rigour through an extended analysis of the interrelated strands of culture, race and racial prejudice in the case at bar. It is sufficient to say that these subjects should have been considered by the court below [the B.C. Supreme Court], and that they weigh in favour of [Elijah] living with the [Edwards family]. They are not, however, determinative."

When Madam Justice Newbury ruled in favour of

Theodore Edwards and cited race as a factor but not a "determinative" one, she provoked numerous angry reactions. For example, the *Vancouver Sun* asserted, in an article on June 30, 2000, "The Supreme Court of Canada will review the decision that awarded custody of Blue Edwards's child by a Coquitlam woman to the former Vancouver Grizzlies player on the basis that the boy is black." The paragraph was grossly misleading. Madam Justice Newbury examined various factors in making her ruling, including each parent's background, character, personality, family environment, and parenting ability. All of that was conveniently ignored in a line that could lead an uninformed reader to conclude, "This is a terrible case of discrimination. The father's getting custody just because he is black."

In an earlier editorial on March 15, 2000, the *Sun* had complained about Madam Justice Newbury's remark that it would be in Elijah's best interests to live with people who could nurture his black identity. "The logic is not obvious to us," the *Sun* editorial fumed. "In the U.S., Elijah's racial heritage also includes terribly disproportionate odds he will die violently while still a young man or be jailed. But the greater concern is that as interracial marriages increase in B.C., the physical appearance of a child of mixed heritage may become the deciding factor in granting custody if divorce ensues. The court's emphasis on appearance is troubling."

It is not obvious to me, either, that Elijah will be better off living in the United States. It all depends on how his life unfolds. But I am not offended, as some Canadians are, by the suggestion that he might be better off living in black American culture. I think the idea bothers Canadians because we like to feel that our culture is morally superior and less laden with racism. But I don't feel that either assertion is true. I look at

Elijah's circumstances, not at him as property of Canada, and I am willing to consider the argument that he might be better off raised by Theodore and Valerie Edwards in Charlotte, N.C., than by his mother in Vancouver, B.C. The quality of care that he would receive in either environment must be the primary deciding factor. The ability to which his black identity—a fragile creature in either country—will be nurtured and supported has to be considered if we truly care about his best interests. It does not, however, have to predominate.

. . .

After Kimberly Van de Perre lost in the B.C. Court of Appeal, her lawyer, Steven Mansfield, persuaded the Supreme Court of Canada to hear the case. He specifically asked the Supreme Court to consider this question: "What role should race play in decisions regarding custody of children of mixed-race relationships? What principles ought to be applied, and were those principles correctly applied in the case at bar?"

The combination of Madam Justice Newbury's written remarks about race and Mansfield's direct question to the Supreme Court of Canada guaranteed strong media coverage of the case by the time it was heard in Ottawa. And it was indeed a precedent-setting case, because it was the first time that Canada's highest court had been asked to rule about whether race should tip the scales in a custody fight.

As of result of the case's importance, the African Canadian Legal Clinic, the Association of Black Social Workers, and the Jamaican Canadian Association asked for and received permission to make written and oral submissions to the Supreme Court of Canada. This, to me, was a good sign. It suggested that a thoughtful discussion of the issue of racial identity—and specifically, how each parent might be able to nurture Elijah Van de Perre's racial identity—might actually take place in court. However, events inside and outside the court on June 14, 2001, showed me that I had been dreaming in Technicolor. The word "race" would crop up a number of times in the court hearing, but few wanted to hold the hot potato and actually examine it.

In media scrums in the lobby of the Supreme Court building, Theodore Edwards told reporters that his ex-lover had spoken negatively to Elijah about black people. Kimberly Van de Perre, for her part, insisted that she loved her son and wanted to live with him. Amidst bright lights, jostling cameramen, and extended microphones, however, neither of them had the opportunity to speak in any depth about the actual welfare of their son, or about the issue of his racial identity.

In court, Steven Mansfield was first to address the nine white justices. He mentioned that the twenty-six–day custody trial at the B.C. Supreme Court had heard from fourteen lay witnesses and two experts, and that 3,500 pages of evidence had been submitted to the B.C. Court of Appeal. Mansfield noted that although lawyers on both sides of the dispute had not dealt with the issue of race in their written submissions to either of the two lower courts, the B.C. Court of Appeal judges introduced the issue of race and the consideration of what role it plays in custody disputes involving a mixed-race child. Although Mansfield had originally asked the Supreme Court of Canada to consider the question of race, he quickly dismissed the issue as irrelevant to Elijah Van de Perre. Each parent had to be evaluated in terms of how they would support Elijah, Mansfield said, arguing that the boy was different from his father *and* from his mother, and that the race factor did not weigh in favour of Theodore Edwards.

The two lawyers for Theodore Edwards complained at length that the B.C. Supreme Court judge who presided over the custody trial had resorted to racial stereotypes in arriving at negative conclusions about Edwards. But neither of them explored the issue of Elijah's mixed-race identity, or how that might be factored into a consideration of his best interests.

Mr. Justice Ian Binnie interrupted Barbara Bulmer, a lawyer for Theodore Edwards, to say that the court couldn't consider race in the absence of evidence indicating that complications had arisen from Elijah Van de Perre's ethnicity. At that point, Chief Justice Beverley McLachlin stepped in. "Before we embark on this very difficult issue, we should have some evidence," she said. "I don't mean to put this in as evidence, but someone told me that either this year or next year Caucasians will be a minority in the city of Vancouver. I just raise that to say that this may be a complicated matter on which it might be dangerous to draw conclusions in the absence of the evidence." The chief justice went on to express doubts as to whether race should be a major factor for consideration by the judges.

It is difficult to know exactly why Chief Justice McLachlin speculated about the diminishing majority of whites in Vancouver, or what she felt it had to do with determining Elijah Van de Perre's best interests. Perhaps she meant to suggest that the black aspects of Elijah's identity wouldn't be a big deal in a city where white people were about to lose their majority status. If that is indeed what she meant, it must be countered that the challenges involved in encouraging Elijah to develop a healthy sense of his own blackness have nothing to do with whether whites account for 51 or 49 per cent of Vancouver's population, and everything to do with the racism so deeply entrenched in Canadian society.

The last lawyer to bring arguments to the Supreme Court was the only legal professional—apart from Madam Justice Mary Newbury of the B.C. Court of Appeal—to grapple with Elijah's racial identity and what it meant in this custody dispute. Representing the African Canadian Legal Clinic, the Jamaican Canadian Association, and the Association of Black Social Workers, Sheena Scott did not say whether Elijah's custody should be awarded to his mother or his father. She did, however, insist that race should be an important factor in determining the best interests of the boy.

"It is because of societally imposed stereotypes, barriers, and prejudices based on skin colour that race is a social reality for the child of African-Canadian parentage and Caucasian parentage. Historically, these children took on the status of the black parent and became part of the black community." In the past, Scott told the judges, white skin was viewed as pure, and a child with any black blood was viewed as tainted. "It is not a question of whether the child is black or white or both, but rather it is about how to nurture and acknowledge the whole child, including the black side of the child, because that is the part that needs protecting," she said. Race takes on an increasingly significant role as a child ages and begins to negotiate a sense of self in more complex relationships, she said, adding that group affiliation is an integral part of identity formation. "The development of a strong sense of racial pride means an offsetting of racism and an affirming of group and self identity. Biracial children being part of both worlds have a heightened need to reconcile these worlds and form a healthy racial identity, including pride in their African-Canadian heritage and overcoming internalized stereotypes about part of who they are."

Scott's arguments, which were augmented by a forty-page written submission that included specific suggestions to encourage a positive sense of racial identity among mixed-race children, elicited nothing but a few skeptical queries from the judges—notably, Madam Justice Claire L'Heureux-Dubé. First, Madam Justice L'Heureux-Dubé asked for reassurance that Scott wasn't advocating that a mixed-race child automatically go with the parent of colour. Scott assured her that she was not calling for "race matching" in child custody cases. "But the way your argument goes," Madam Justice L'Heureux-Dubé insisted, "it almost follows because you say it's very important they know their background, their colour, their culture, whatever. It seems to me that the argument you're making drags us inevitably to the fact that if they have that colour they're better in that environment. So that's what I just wanted to clear up. Where do you go with this?"

"We need to look at how each parent will help make the child's identity complete," Scott replied. When she went on a few moments later to list some of challenges that mixed-race youth can face in coming to terms with the black aspects of their racial identity, Madam Justice L'Heureux-Dubé cut in again. "It's vice-versa," she said. "It is on both sides."

With due respect to Madam Justice L'Heureux-Dubé, the challenges that blacks face in coping with matters of race are not experienced by whites in a "vice-versa" manner. As Emily Carasco, the family law professor and an acknowledged expert in this field, told me in an interview, "There are not too many experiences I can think of that we thrust upon white kids because they're white." But plenty of things—from name calling in the schoolyard to more extreme forms of racism—happen to children specifically because they are black.

In the final analysis, some journalists, lawyers, and judges appear to worry that the case involving Elijah Van de Perre could usher in an era of automatically granting custody of mixed-race children to the parent of colour. The fact is, though, that nobody—or at least, nobody in four years of litigation over Elijah's custody—is calling for that solution. Anybody who bothered to sit down and think about it, or perhaps to read the well-researched factum prepared by the African Canadian Legal Clinic, would see that all that is being sought is a thoughtful discussion of how to serve the best interests of the biracial child.

When Sheena Scott was nearing the end of her presentation, it appeared that although she had deeply felt remarks to deliver, the stage curtain had already fallen in front of her. The lawyers on the two opposing sides had once again managed to avoid discussing the needs of a biracial child. The judges had indicated a strong reluctance to consider the matter. And the journalists were preparing to rush out into the foyer to scrum Theodore Edwards and Kimberly Van de Perre. I am wondering, therefore, if anybody heard Scott's last words in court that day. They bear repeating.

"The literature consistently calls for acute awareness and understanding of the unique issues faced by African-Canadian biracial children, by their parents, teachers, assessors and the court," Scott said. "No parent is expected to be perfect. All parents learn with their children, but the expectations, like the needs, are high. Each parent should be given the opportunity to identify their level of understanding, as well as their past and future plans for dealing with issues related to race. African-Canadian parents have much which they can uniquely offer to the biracial child, in terms of empathy, life experiences, oral history and approaches taken to racism. . . . Historically, African-Canadians have had to prepare their children to negotiate two worlds, whether they're white . . . biracial or black. A Caucasian parent who is aware of racism . . . acknowledges his or her own limitations, including extended family racism, for example, and who seeks out appropriate support such as African-Canadian mentors or other mentors, or who is open to exposing the child in a meaningful way to his racial heritage, also has much to offer."

And there lies the rub. Theodore Edwards probably has the ability to foster a positive sense of racial awareness and identity in his son. Kimberly Van de Perre could do it, too. This case could have included, as part of an overall review of Elijah's best interests, a thoughtful, sane, cool discussion about how either parent could meet those needs. But Canadians, still in denial and believing there is no racism in Canada, no unique needs for biracial children, and no need to have raised this issue in court, have managed to put off the discussion for yet another day.

In a CBC television documentary entitled *Losing Elijah*, which first aired in 2000 and ran again on the evening of the Supreme Court of Canada case, on June 14, 2001, Kimberly Van de Perre told journalist Kathy Tomlinson: "I'm extremely disappointed that the issue of race was ever brought up at all because it's not an issue. He's a beautiful little boy, regardless [of] what colour his skin is."

Welcome to Canada, Elijah. I hope you can make more sense of it than your elders.

Part Three

Sticks
and Stones

The Question

Canadians have a favourite pastime, and they don't even realize it. They like to ask—they absolutely have to ask—where you are from if you don't look convincingly white. They want to know it, need to know it, simply must have that information. They just can't relax until they have pinpointed, to their satisfaction, your geographic and racial coordinates. They can go almost out of their minds with curiosity, as when driven by the need for food, water, or sex, but once they've finally managed to find out precisely where you were born, who your parents were, and what your racial make-up is, then, man, do they feel better. They can breathe easy and get back to the business of living.

I don't have the math background of, say, an actuary, but I can manage the following calculation. I am forty-four years old. Since about age ten, I have been asked "So what are you, anyway?" and all its variations. ("Where are you from?" "Yes, but where are you really from?" "Yes, but where were your parents born?") That's thirty-four years I've been fielding The Question.

Let's assume I have been asked The Question once a day over these past thirty-four years. $34 \times 365 = 12{,}410$. But that would be an underestimation because it fails to factor in the two years I lived in Quebec. During those two years, I was most certainly asked The Question five times per day. (*"D'où viens-tu?"* *"Quelles sont tes souches?"* *"Tes parents sont de quel pays?"*) An extra four times per day for two years in Quebec City would add on another 2,920 questions. 12,410 + 2,920 = 15,330.

That, ladies and gentlemen, is the absolute minimum number of times Canadians have asked me either "Where are you from?" or *"D'où viens-tu?"* or any of the multitudinous variations.

Minelle Mahtani, whose doctoral thesis at the University of London examined identity among mixed-race Canadian women, tells a story of how she was walking alone one day in Toronto's St. Lawrence Market area, when someone tapped on her shoulder. Minelle turned around to find a woman who seemed motivated by a particular urgency—she had obviously been watching Minelle and just had to know where she was from.

"Ah," you may say, "but it's just curiosity. What's wrong with people being curious?"

I am a patient man. So patient that my children can confidently remove a chocolate chip cookie right from the edge of my fingers, or raid my dish of French vanilla ice cream and leave nothing but the cloudy bowl, and still know that I won't lose my cool. But even this patience was exhausted some time around the 5,000 mark of the 15,330 questions I have faced.

What is wrong with The Question? Nothing at all—when it is asked at the right time, when it results from a genuine interest in you as a person, and when the person asking the question actually accepts the answer.

Let's dissect the interrogation process. Imagine me at a party, sipping mineral water. A stranger walks up.

STRANGER: "Do you mind my asking where you are from?" [This is code for "What is your race?"]

ME: "Canada." [This is code for "Screw off."]

STRANGER : "Yes, but you know, where are you *really* from?" [This is code for "You know what I mean, so why are you trying to make me come out and say it?"]

ME: "I come from the foreign and distant metropolis of Newmarket. That's Newmarket, Ontario. My place of birth. [Code for "I'm not letting you off the hook, buster."]

STRANGER: "But your place of origin? Your parents? What are your parents?" [Code for "I want to know your race, but this is making me very uncomfortable because somehow I feel that I'm not supposed to ask that question."]

This exchange is like the opening of a chess game. The first few moves are pretty standard: White moves Pawn to King Four, Black responds with Pawn to King Four, White answers with Knight to King Bishop Three, and Black answers with Knight to King Bishop Three. From this point on, the possibilities multiply.

I can give a teaser, such as "My parents came up from the States," which frustrates the questioner, who really wants to know my parents' racial background.

I can give it all up and explain that I have a black father and a white mother.

I can invent an answer, such as "My father is a White Russian and my mother is an Ethiopian Jew."

Or I can turn the question around, as in "Why are you asking me this?"

And that is the nub of the issue. Why am I always asked that question? Why do people need to know the answer so desperately?

Have you ever noticed that black people rarely put other people of any race through the ringer like this? That's because many of them have been asked The Question more times than they care to count. They're sophisticated enough—by virtue of their own experiences—to understand that many people resent this line of interrogation.

Is it truly innocent? Can The Question be chalked up to basic curiosity? I don't think so. Children are the most innocent and curious of all human beings, yet they never hammer me with these questions. As a rule, adults aren't all that curious about other people. With me, they are generally interested in just one thing: my ancestry.

Do you suppose that—15,330 times in thirty-four years—strangers will ask an indisputably white Canadian with a traditional Anglo-Canadian accent where he is from, where he was born, or where his parents were born? Absolutely not. Strangers will assume that he is a true Canadian, and leave that part of his identity unmolested. The offence-causing kernel at the centre of this line of interrogation is its implication: "You are not white, you don't look like me, so you're clearly not Canadian." It also suggests "Since you're clearly not Canadian, and I am, I am within my rights to ask you just exactly where you're from."

We grow up learning that certain questions are off-limits in polite conversation. Any properly socialized Canadian knows, by the teenage years at the latest, that it would be considered grossly impolite to walk up to strangers and ask how much money they make, how they vote, whether they believe in God, or whether they sleep with men, women, or both. These questions are deemed intrusive. But to my way of thinking, they are eminently preferable to "Where are you from?" After all, what is wrong with asking what people do or think? But to ask what they *are*, and to presume to know at least part of the answer—that they are not white and therefore are not Canadian—is very different.

Digging into someone's identity—especially a stranger's identity—is tricky business. Hell, people can spend top dollar on psychotherapists to figure out their own identities and still fall short of satisfaction. When I wake up in the morning, stumble to the mirror, and brush my teeth, I'm certainly not saying to myself, "Hello, black man, how are you today?" Nor am I saying, "Hello, white and black mix-up, what are you doing today?"

Obviously, the blackness and the whiteness within me are reflected back at me by society. But I don't care to have my identity boiled down to race. My identity may, at any given time, comprise a hundred elements.

I suppose the reason many of us mixed-race people find The Question offensive is not just that it makes assumptions, which are often false, about our identity, but because it attempts to hang our identity on one factor: our race.

• • •

Not everybody I interviewed had the same take on this issue. Interestingly, two of the strongest opposing views came from young men, both in their twenties, university-educated, and living in southern Ontario.

Stefan Dubowski, of Hamilton, told me The Question doesn't bother him. When he is asked about his background, he just says he is part Ukrainian, part Barbadian. "Then we get into a discussion of what they thought I was. I've had Armenian, Egyptian, Pakistani, East Indian . . . It's just a question of curiosity. I've been asked so many times.

If I got mad about it every single time, I'd just be this really angry person. I certainly don't feel any anger about it when people ask me about it, but my back does go up when I read it on an application form or on a government census."

Tyson Brown, who was raised in Burlington and now lives in Toronto, said he takes The Question as an opportunity to educate people about issues of mixed race and blackness. "I say, 'I'm mixed, African Canadian and white Canadian.'" Tyson emerged from a largely white high school to embrace his black identity completely as a young man. He read black literature, listened to black music, wore funky black clothes, dated black women, and chose to immerse himself completely in the black student community at York University. Later, he lived with his girlfriend for a year in Barbados, and there the constant references to his race grated on him. "They called me 'red man' the whole time I was there," he complained.

However, my brother, Dan, described The Question as a painful experience, especially during childhood. "I was definitely asked that question a lot. And a lot of times, when I said part black, or half black, people would then decide to argue with me and tell me that no, I wasn't, 'cause I didn't look black enough. I can remember it happening a lot when I was a boy, at summer camp. When I went up to camp for the first time, I was sitting on the bus with this kid who was probably a year or two older than I was. And this kid was saying, 'You're not. You can't be.' So there I was arguing with him about this."

Like Dan, most of the people I interviewed—and virtually all of the women—expressed impatience with constant questions about their racial background.

Karyn Hood, of Toronto, said, "People think I'm everything under the flipping sun, and it drives me insane. I get

North African, Moroccan, Italian, Sicilian, Greek, Spanish, Jewish . . . Whenever I meet someone, I know it's going to be 'What are you? What background are you?' I usually try to put it to bed with one answer: 'My father is West Indian, my mother's Irish Canadian.' It's annoying. But life's a puzzle, and they want to know how you fit into their world." Karyn resents being perceived as "exotic," cultivates friendships in the black community, and prefers to date black men. "You can't live in two worlds. You have to make a choice. Saying you're white isn't really an option. So this makes it clear to people. If there's any doubt, that's the choice I'm making."

Natalie Wall, of Toronto, concurred. "I've been asked what I am so many times. It is the rudest question in the world. It's the basest form of labelling I've ever seen. People on the street are always guessing. 'You're Spanish, right? Indian? What the hell are you?' I tell them I'm Canadian. 'But where are you from?' 'Canada.' 'What about your parents?' 'My mom is from Nova Scotia, my dad is from Trinidad.' 'So what are you?' 'Black.' I get a surprised look. 'You *are*?'"

Jazz Miller, of Toronto, is so sick of The Question that when people ask her what she is, she has taken to answering "aardvark." "It is designed to embarrass the person asking the question. There's always a little bit of nervous laughter."

Aaron Cavon, who has a white father and a black mother, was a graduate student at Dalhousie University when I interviewed him. He said people always look astonished when he says that The Question irritates him and he won't answer it. He described the attitude of the questioner as unconsciously aggressive, a stance that suggests the person being questioned is inferior. Underneath The Question, Aaron argued, is this unarticulated belief: "It's not necessary for me to explain my origins, but it's necessary for you to tell me who you are." He told me, "The assumption behind The Question is, 'I'm just white. You are the person who answers the question because you are the one who is unknown.'"

Sara, one of my anonymous interviewees, fumed as she recalled the numerous times she had dealt with The Question.

"Sometimes I'm very rude. I don't give much information. I might just say, 'I'm from here.' Some days, if I don't feel like it, I just say, 'Africa.' And they're happy, not realizing that Africa's a continent and that there are fifty-two countries in it. It's just what they want to hear. They want to place you somewhere because it makes them feel comfortable, helps them compartmentalize you.

"Where the hell are they from? No one's from here unless they're First Nations peoples. But they're trying to make you feel strange. It's a displacement. They're just trying to let you know that you don't belong . . . They are not coming from a position of intelligence, asking those questions. White privilege doesn't operate from a level of consciousness. It operates from a position of privilege. Because they're privileged, they don't have to think about stuff. They really don't. Does it mean that they're not well intentioned? These can be people you love dearly, you know? But that's the way the world is. They're operating from a position of belligerent white privilege, and they don't have to look at stuff and think about stuff. So they ask these reckless questions."

The N-Word

My parents are atheists. I knew so little about religions when I was young that I shocked a friend's mother one day by asking her who that man was in her wall portrait, and why he was stuck and bleeding on the T-shaped logs. Sunday, in my family, was a day for me to clean the bathroom, wash the kitchen floor, sweep the garage, cut the grass, and then snatch up my homemade go-kart while the church-going neighbours dressed their children in jackets and ties and packed them into station wagons. Nothing in the world tasted sweeter than holding them up for a few seconds as I ran the go-kart past their driveway, bobsled-style, then jumped aboard and bombed down our street, which was set on a big hill.

Despite our household's lack of religion, other moral codes prevailed, and some quite seriously. My mother, for example, introduced a few specific prohibitions. Most had to do with foods that were verboten: South African products coming from the apartheid regime; the Aunt Jemima pancake mix for its portrait of a happy slave; any products from Portugal, which at the time was still run by a brutal military dictatorship; and California grapes because we were backing a strike by Cesar Chavez and his Latin American fruit pickers. My mother continues to boycott products from various countries. She curses the Canadian government for re-establishing contacts so quickly with China after the Tiananmen Square massacre of 1989. To this day, she is so disgusted by ongoing human rights abuses that she won't buy any product made in China.

One family code that came down from both parents was absolute and unrelenting: "Thou shalt not let the word 'nigger' pass without the strongest objection."

Raining my fists down on the heads of those uttering the words was the solution that my father proposed, in his own subtle way. He told countless stories of his childhood, walking to school every morning through an Italian-American neighbourhood in Portland, Oregon, and having to hand over his glasses once or twice daily to his little sister while he engaged in fisticuffs with some boy who had shouted out a racial taunt.

But I am not a physically aggressive man, so fighting has never been a viable option for me. The first time I tried it, I met with disaster. I was about ten years old and had been called "nigger" in the playground. Gentleman pugilist that I was, I arranged to meet the boy after school, just a hundred yards from my house. I had a sense that I would be beaten, and I did not want twenty-three other children circling us, stomping feet, clapping hands, and urging us on with "Fight, fight, fight." I had seen this happen a number of times before, and I had always pitied the loser. I don't remember my opponent's name. Let's call him Carl. He had straight brown hair, and I remember wondering, as he came at me, whether he would have used the word "nigger" if his hair had been curly. If his hair had been curly, I reasoned, one of his distant ancestors might have been black. But Carl hadn't come for a philosophical discussion. We rumbled, pushed, and shoved, and I didn't like the feeling because his arms and his chest seemed stronger than mine. I was the faster runner, but running wouldn't work because I'd still have to face him the next day. So I had to fight.

I threw an undercut at his stomach because I'd seen that move on *Superman* once, but he popped me on the nose, leaving me with a dull, throbbing ache and the worry that my nose might end up looking flatter than it already did. I didn't like my hair so frizzy, and I wanted my nose more aquiline, and this fight was certainly taking cosmetic surgery in the wrong direction. I punched and shoved again, and got myself hit once or twice more in the nose—*damn*, did that hurt!—and the mouth. Was I going to get a tooth knocked out? I had seen children with teeth knocked out, and the open and gaping hole struck me as ugly, low class, and uneducated. I couldn't let that happen to me—the flat nose was already enough to deal with. I jostled and slapped with arms extended to remove myself from the range of Carl's fists. I recall more about his body—bigger than mine, stronger—and his breathing—loud, laboured, grunting—than I do about his face. I did not want to look into the eyes of the boy that I was fighting, and more than anything else I desired to remove myself from the deteriorating situation. Fortunately, a school crossing guard had finished her duty and was walking our way.

"Hey," she called out, "stop that."

"All right, all right," I told him. "Let's call it a tie." He was good with his fists, this boy, but slower with words, so I pressed on. "We won't do this again, and I won't make you fight again and get you in trouble, if you don't use that word again. All right. You got that?"

I raised my voice for the benefit of the approaching crossing guard, whose name, coincidentally, was Mrs. Hill, although she was no relation of mine, because she was white—as white as could be—and about a thousand years old. Anyway, Mrs. Hill, combined with my verbal footwork, seemed to save the day. Carl and I backed away from each other. As I walked home, touching my lips and nose to gauge the flow of blood, I began rehearsing the line, "Yeah, but you should have seen what I did to him."

Fighting in or out of the schoolyard over the word "nigger" never worked for me. I was scrawny, no better than average height, and had no idea how to do it. I tried it only once or twice more and then abandoned the practice. Even when I once won a fight—this time with a boy in my grade five class who chose in his wisdom to call me a nigger and a Nazi in the same breath—it felt like a hollow, ugly victory, and I stopped the instant the boy started crying. In any case, most of the times I heard the word "nigger," fisticuffs simply weren't an option. The speaker would have been an eleven-year-old white girl in pigtails and a blue dress who was deciding at recess which one of us would be "it" for tag:

Eenie meenie miney mo
Catch a nigger by the toe
If he hollers let him go
Eenie meenie miney mo

The disgraceful and disgusting image didn't escape me, even at that age. I remember wondering, Does this child see what she is saying? In her mind, does she picture what the words describe? Can she not see the image of people chasing down a black man like a dog or a rat, snaring him by the toe just for sport; listening with amusement to his hollering, and then releasing him to run wild again, like "other" forest animals?

Even with his warnings about combating the N-word, my father would have killed me for fighting an eleven-year-old white girl in pigtails and a blue dress. So what was I to do? I started avoiding tag games. When I was drawn into them, I would insist on being the one who determined who was to be "it." And as I called out the rhyme, I substituted "tiger" for "nigger":

Eenie meenie miney mo
Catch a tiger by the toe
If he hollers let him go
Eenie meenie miney mo

No place in the world seems more rampant with social politics, moral judgements, and the market forces of friendship than the public school playground. Everybody knows who has friends, who lacks them, who is deserving of attention and who is not, and where exactly everyone fits in. I was certainly not going to destroy my own finely wrought social status by alienating every white kid present—virtually every other kid in the school except my brother and sister—by getting into a long argument about why they had no business using the word "nigger."

But today, not standing up to people who use the word "nigger," or to people who engage in more subtle forms of racism, seems the ultimate violation of a family sacrament. It unlocks feelings of self-loathing. I now feel bound to respond if somebody says something repugnant, especially along racial lines. If I don't, I hate myself for lacking courage.

My brother, Dan, who is two years older, completely understands the nature of our family code. He referred in our interview to a scene in Newmarket, a town just north of Toronto, where our family lived until 1960. The incident took place when Dan was five or six years old.

"I remember that there were some very racist cartoons depicting blacks as savages, gripping bones in their teeth, this sort of horrible caricature, and I took either Mom or Dad to the TV and asked who they were," Dan told me. "I wasn't sure if they were animals, or humans, or some kind of combination thereof, and my father immediately turned off the TV and said, 'That's them making fun of blacks, showing blacks in a very ugly, horrible light, and by doing that, they're making fun of you. Therefore, you're not allowed to watch this channel anymore.' Then Dad turned around and wrote letters of complaint, demanding that the show be taken off the air, and I would sometimes go to my friends' houses and watch those shows there. Hearing that, Dad was very upset, and I think Mom had said at one point he cried, he was so upset that I was still watching the show. There was this sense of his pride in being black, his fury at racist images. He would caution me to watch people who were making racist comments about anybody— for example, the neighbours. He said if they used 'wop' to describe an Italian, you'd better believe they were gonna use 'nigger' to describe you when you weren't around. And that, again, was his indirect way of circling the wagons and saying, 'You have to have pride in yourself. Have pride in who you are, and don't condone racist remarks about anyone, because in doing that, you're showing a lack of belief in yourself at the same time and a lack of respect for your race.' "

Dan went on to mention that, as a child, he felt pressure to oppose people who said something racist. But he often didn't take them on, which made him feel guilty. I said that

I still felt that way. He responded, "It probably resonates with a lot of stuff from childhood, where I sat silently. I think, as an adult, if you hear something like that, well, the first reason you're reacting is 'cause it's wrong and should be corrected, but at least in my case, the second reason is compensation for not doing it as a child."

• • •

The word "nigger" wasn't limited to the schoolyards and playgrounds of my childhood. I also found it in books and slowly developed a sense of literary contexts in which the word might be used appropriately. For example, I discovered the N-word and other troubling reflections of racism in the works of the American writer Langston Hughes, whose anger and poignancy leapt off the page. In "Cross," Hughes wrote:

> My old man died in a fine big house
> My ma died in a shack
> I wonder where I'm gonna die
> Being neither white nor black?

And in "Mulatto," Hughes used a sharper blade. Let me quote one stanza from the poem:

> The moon over the turpentine woods.
> The Southern night
> Full of stars,
> Great big yellow stars.
>   What's a body but a toy?
>   Juicy bodies
>   Of nigger wenches
>   Blue black

> Against black fences
> O, you little bastard boy,
> What's a body but a toy?
> The scent of pine wood stings the soft night air
> *What's the body of your mother?*
> Silver moonlight everywhere.
> *What's the body of your mother?*
> Sharp pine scent in the evening air.
> A nigger night,
> A nigger joy,
> A little yellow
> Bastard boy.

Interestingly, Hughes—who was born in 1902 in Joplin, Missouri, and raised in poverty before he emerged as the first black American poet to achieve international fame—insisted on the comic in his writing. He loved the blues (I even own a tape of him reciting his own written poetry to blues played by the jazzman Charles Mingus) but he sometimes cut his own words with humour. In 1953, in the foreword to *Simple Stakes a Claim*, Hughes wrote: "If Negroes took all the white world's daily boorishness to heart and wept over it as profoundly as our serious writers do, we would have been dead long ago ... The race problem in America is serious business, I admit. But must it *always* be written about seriously?"

In his poem "Mulatto," however, Hughes wrote with blood boiling and used the word "nigger" to perfectly livid effect.

The word—with its variations of meaning—simply refuses to die. These days, you hear black kids calling each other "nigger" in the streets by way of playful salutation. And the word pops up constantly in rap music, which originates in urban counterculture and aims to speak for disenfranchised black youths. Hip-hop artists use a lot of other nasty words, too—especially ones that denigrate women. But I don't accept "nigger" or any of their sexist terms. Bottom line? The N-word irritates me and irritates some other blacks, too. And when we hear whites parroting self-deprecating blackspeak, it becomes downright absurd. Ivan Gibbs, of Montreal, complained to me about hearing white kids approach each other on the street wearing baggy pants falling down over their backsides and greeting each other with "Whassup, my nigger?" Ivan wondered whether they had any idea how ridiculous they looked.

I, for one, refuse to take the word "nigger" lying down, even if it is used by black people within black culture. It is a word that slave-owning profiteers slapped down on my ancestors. It represents distilled hatred in its purest form. To me, there is no single word in the English language that embodies more hatred than "nigger." It is not a word I'm going to ignore. From time to time, the word is used to political effect, as Langston Hughes used it in "Mulatto." But you won't catch me slapping some brother's hand at a party and calling out, "Whassup, my nigger?" Nor will I ever use "nigga"—another common hip-hop term. I've actually seen a Web site devoted to discussing the differences between "nigger" and "nigga." But as far as I'm concerned, they mean the same thing. They have the same history. You can't slide out from under the history and heft of a word by touching up its last syllable.

The word "nigger," with its ghastly history, has insinuated itself into my own life. It always takes me back to the "Eenie meenie miney mo" rhyme that punctuated the schoolyards of my childhood. For me, and for so many of the people interviewed for this book, "nigger" was the word of choice for children and adults who wanted to say that they hated us, that we did not belong, and that we never would. To this day, "nigger" will not leave us alone. It refuses to disappear. Even when it is not in your face, you know that at an unexpected moment it may leap out at you. But are there times when using the word is, if not laudable, at least justifiable?

When I was writing this chapter, I got on the phone with the owner of a lovely bed-and-breakfast in Niagara-on-the-Lake, Ontario. It is a gorgeous and wealthy community, and one steeped in black history. I was going there to speak to members of this woman's book club during February, which is Black History Month. (I can never help thinking how ironic it is that Black History Month is the shortest month of the year. Twenty-eight cold days. *Damn*.) The bed-and-breakfast owner had arranged for a local historian to give us a walking tour of the black history sites in town. But first, she wanted to know if book club members could clear up some matters of terminology with me.

"And what might they be?" I asked.

"The guide says that the section of town where the blacks lived was always referred to as Nigger Town."

She wanted to know if it was okay to use that phrase. My answer was that people had no business tossing the word around indiscriminately, but at the same time, it was important to acknowledge that black people were once referred to this way. When I arrived a few days later to take part in the walking tour, the guide proved knowledgeable about black history in Niagara-on-the-Lake. She spoke for an hour or two about where blacks had lived, what kind of jobs they had held, whom they had married, and how they had escaped American slave catchers. It seemed important for her to contend that the black people of Niagara-on-the-Lake had not faced racism. Indeed, she said, a number of black men in the town's history had married white women. She seemed oblivious to the irony that she was delivering these very words in a neighbourhood once dubbed Nigger Town.

I was recently asked to write the introduction to a children's novella entitled *Underground to Canada* by the Canadian author Barbara Smucker. The book tells the story of two young black girls escaping from American slavery and making their way north to St. Catharines, Ontario. It was first published in 1977. Penguin Books Canada told me that some people had objected to the book's use of the word "nigger." Apparently, some educators who had otherwise liked the book had even contacted the publisher to ask if it would be possible to reissue Smucker's novel minus the offending N-word.

There is no doubt that teachers—especially those of relatively young children—face huge challenges teaching literature that contains the word. From time to time, parents and educators also object to *Huckleberry Finn* for the same reason. In the early 1980s, when I was a newspaper reporter for the *Winnipeg Free Press*, I wrote an article about a Winnipeg section of the now-defunct National Black Coalition of Canada, which wanted the book removed from school classrooms because of the character Nigger Jim. Without question, literature that raises painful social issues is also difficult to teach. But literature isn't meant to be pretty. It isn't written to make people feel good about themselves. My eleven-year-old daughter was recently introduced to *The Diary of Anne Frank*. No one would call that book a joyous literary experience, but she is learning from it, and possibly becoming a more aware, thinking human being as a result.

Teaching books that make use of the word "nigger" must be difficult, but in the case of *Underground to Canada*, there was really no getting away from it. Smucker could hardly have recreated slave owners' dialogue without the word, and the language her characters use reflects the era in which the story unfolds. It was Smucker's job to write a fine children's novel, and she acquitted herself well. It is the job of parents and teachers to explain the book to children, to work with them to ensure that their knowledge grows as a result of reading it, and to set the scenes and the language of the book into a meaningful social and historical context.

In that case, I wouldn't advise running from the word "nigger." I would advise walking straight up to the baseball plate, gripping the bat with all of our knowledge and intelligence, locking our eyes onto the word, and taking a good hard swing when it comes at us.

Since my childhood, it seems that everybody has been taking the N-word and either throwing it, catching it, or swinging at it. My first playful encounter with the word was when I was given the book *Nigger*, by the black American comedian Dick Gregory. This book tried to yank all of the sting out of the word by making it hilarious and by lobbing one absurdity after another at the reader. For example, Gregory described one scene in which a waiter refused him service, but apologized for not being allowed to serve coloured people. Gregory shot back that it was okay because he didn't eat them anyway, and much preferred chicken.

"Nigger" definitely rolls off the tongue in a different way, and carries a different meaning, when it comes from the mouth of a black person. It is allowed because it is coming from inside the culture. If you don't believe me, devise your own little test. Send two friends of yours—one black and one white—up to a black man in a bar, and have each person ask him, "Whassup, nigger?" One of those friends may get a handshake. The other may end up in the nearest emergency ward.

Blacks folks can strut around and shoot off the N-word, or so the thinking goes, because it's ours and we're taking it back, just as some gays have reappropriated "fag" and "queer" and some lesbians have chosen to assert themselves with the word "dyke."

But one woman I interviewed, Suzette Mayr of Calgary, disagreed with this approach. Suzette, a novelist, poet, and English teacher at the Alberta College of Art and Design, made the point that for her—a lesbian and a person of mixed race—the words "queer" and "dyke" don't carry nearly the emotional wallop of "nigger." She said, "I don't like it, but I understand the idea. You take the word and reappropriate it to make it less harmful."

Like Suzette, I can't see myself settling into a tranquil acceptance of "nigger" in this lifetime. But I do understand the inclination to remove the sting from a word by using it over and over. And there is something to be said for the idea that repetition dulls the senses. Incredible as this may seem, Jazz Miller, of Toronto, told me that her white mother called her "nigger" repeatedly when she was a young child in order to desensitize her to the word. Her mother thought that it would then hurt less when some idiot in the school-yard threw the word in Jazz's face. Jazz looks back with indulgence on her mother's parenting technique and says it worked, but she acknowledges that she wouldn't use the strategy on her own son.

Nicole Bernhardt, who is in her first year of studies at Queen's University and was born to a black mother and a white father, had this to say about the N-word: "I don't like it. It doesn't send shivers down my spine, and it doesn't strike me as being so odd in a song, but I don't like it." Nicole said that she sometimes listens to rap music and can relax and enjoy it, but that on the whole she has turned away from it. "I have numerous problems with rap music because of its violence and because it is degrading to women. When I do listen to it, it's with a grain of salt."

I have always taught my three children that every word has its particular weight, and that you have to learn how and when to throw it. No word is out of bounds. Even the most vile and crude word may serve its purpose. "Please" and "thank you" won't buy any safety if somebody is coming after you in a back alley. I'm not one to ban words or books. Indeed, I have used "nigger" in my own writing—in dialogue where it was required. So, I say, know the history and the weight of the N-word. Use it consciously, proceed with caution—and don't ask me to jump on the reappropriation bandwagon.

Forty-Eight Parts White

In 1974, I flew to Washington, D.C., to visit my paternal grandparents. They lived in a house in a middle-class part of town. Their winding road stretched up a long hill and along a lovely park. My grandparents must have been among the only black folks left on the street. Family legend has it that many more black families had once resided there, but they had been bounced out of the neighbourhood for failing to pay, or not knowing to pay, their property taxes.

It took my grandmother, May, about two minutes to unlock her door, slide back three deadbolts, and let me in. "How on earth did you get here, son?" She gave me a hug, kissed me three times, and slammed and bolted the door. She nearly died when I told her that I had taken a series of buses from the airport. She went on for a few minutes about how it was a miracle I hadn't been mugged, robbed, and left for dead. I mumbled something about how the ride wasn't much more eventful than taking city buses in Toronto, except that there were a lot more black people down here and I liked that.

May then said something that sounded as if it could have come straight out of my father's mouth: "Yes, black people are fine, mighty fine, as long as they don't knock you upside your head."

The essence of this comment, reiterated so many times during my childhood, was that I should care for black people, respect them, do good things for them, never speak badly about them in public, and realize that I was connected to them by community—but that I'd be a damn fool to let down my guard and trust them!

May was about seventy-five years old, and she still read a book a day. She had survived throat cancer, and had a burnt-out, reddish-orange patch of radiated flesh in the middle of her throat. She never made any attempt to cover it up or apologize for it. Her uncommon beauty seemed to me to be enhanced by that mark of her victory over cancer. Her voice was raspy, but she walked with strength and determination, without any walking aids, and she had a strong, firm handshake and beautiful brown, slender, long, almost wrinkle-free fingers, although arthritis had bent them.

May's comment had got me thinking about people's attitudes toward black people and questions of terminology. I asked her straight out, "Have you ever heard anyone use the term 'freedom fighter,' instead of 'slave'?"

She scoffed. "Well, they *were* slaves, which is why they were escaping to the northern States and to Canada. *Freedom fighters!* They sure weren't thinking of themselves as freedom fighters. They were other people's property, son—chattel, like horses, pigs, and cows. I don't much see the point in changing the word now to make people feel better about the past."

This response made me consider other terms, such as "coloured," "negro," and "black." What term, I asked May, did she use when thinking of herself?

"Son, I am an Afro-American."

I just about fell off my chair. This was 1974, and I had never heard such a term before.

"I don't care for those other words," May went on to say. "Afro-American is how I like to refer to myself."

I was struck by the decisiveness with which May reached out in a new direction, given that she wasn't satisfied with the choice of words that society was offering her. She helped me to understand that people have a right to say, "Forget this, I'm taking that instead," when it comes to terminology used to describe them. And why not? Why should black people put up with names or descriptions that don't suit them?

· · ·

Over the past thirty or so years, the terms used to describe black people have evolved from "coloured people" to "Negro," "black," "Afro-Canadian," "African-Canadian," and even, for some, "people of colour." These days, I just use "black," but only because nothing better seems to be kicking around.

The utter inadequacy of racial terminology plagues us to this day. Why? Because racial definitions themselves are meaningless. The absurdity becomes most obvious—and the situation would be funny if only people didn't take it so seriously—when describing people of mixed race. A few thousand times already, I've heard people start a sentence this way: "I've got this friend who is half black and half white, and the other day she . . ."

Whoa. Stop right there. Let's roll out the linguistascope and look this one over. *Half black, half white*. Hmm. I've performed tests on myself, scratched my skin, measured my legs, taken blood samples, evaluated colour schemes, but I just can't locate a black half and a white half. My blood isn't either colour, actually, which makes things even more confusing.

Racial categorization seems like a science. But it's not. It's a pseudo-science, built on myth and misinformation. Just look at the language: one-half black, one-quarter black, one-eighth. Thanks in no small part to these descriptions, some people actually end up believing racial identity can be quantified. All one has to do is glance at one's parents and grandparents, run some quick arithmetic, and *voilà*. But nothing could be further from the truth.

Let's look at some of the terminology we've come up with over the years.

If you've got two white parents, you're white. In this case, you can breathe easy. You're safe—you hope. You never know, actually. Some rude genealogist might jump down from a tree and announce that your grandmother was black. If that happens, all bets are off. If you've got any known black blood, you're black. After all, somebody had to take the seats in the segregated buses. Somebody had to do the work, build the plantations, pick the cotton, clean up white babies. That's just the way of the world.

Okay, we're clear so far. We've got white people. That's easy. And we've got black people. That's ... well, pretty easy. They're people with any black blood, even if five thousand other ancestors were white. But now we get into the gradations of blackness. Here comes the tricky part.

If you have one black and one white parent, you're a mulatto. That doesn't make you any less black, but you're a mulatto nonetheless. Nice. Very nice. Lovely etymology. My heart fills with pride. Open a decent dictionary and you'll find that "mulatto" comes from the Spanish *mulo*, for mule. A mule, in case you're a city person and don't know any better, is the offspring of a donkey and a horse. According to the *Oxford Shorter Dictionary on Historical Principles*, here are two other ways that "mule" has been defined over the years: (a) A stupid or obstinate person; (b) One who is "neither one thing nor the other."

Well, it may not be pretty, but at least it's straightforward. A mulatto has one black and one white parent. Next, please.

Quadroon. That's a person who has one white and one mulatto parent.

Octoroon. A person with one white and one quadroon parent. Still with me?

If you've got two mulatto parents, that makes you a cascos.

Mulatto plus black makes you a sambo. Oh, lovely. Sambo, for those of you unfamiliar with the children's story, was a black boy who got his butt chased around and around a tree by a tiger. Said tiger disintegrated into a pool of butter, and Sambo licked his chops, collected the butter and took it home to Mama, who made pancakes. A caveat here: If you happen to meet a genuine sambo, I would advise you not to test out the term. You might get your own butt chased around a tree.

Sambo plus black makes you a mango. I was delighted to discover this term, and reassured to know that we can now not only rigorously define black people, but also, if they're ripened, eat them, too. You would be amazed to know how often food images are used to describe gradations of colour among people of mixed race. But let's return to our linguistics course.

If you happen to have octoroon and white parents, you are a mustifee. And if you have mustifee and white parents, you're a mustifino. It gets even more complicated. Courtesy of the good folks of Louisiana, who surely perfected the art of segregation by day and integration by night, we have the words "meamelouc" for a person said to be one-sixteenth African and "sang-mêlé" for a person considered one-sixty-fourth black.

Isn't it intellectually exhausting to keep all those racial shades in the correct slots, especially given that they are all a myth anyway? If you actually think it makes any sense to speak of a human body as being one-half or one-quarter or one-eighth or one-sixteenth black, you'd better sign up for a high school biology class.

Let me quote briefly from *Who Is Black? One Nation's Definition*, by F. James Davis: "Genes are randomly distributed among individuals ... Having one or more black ancestors does not prove that an individual has some negroid traits or can transmit genes from African forebears. The widely held belief is that an individual's racial traits and genetic carriers are necessarily in direct proportion to the person's fraction of African black ancestry. Some persons with three-eighths or even one-half African lineage have been known to pass as white, presumably in cases in which the number of 'negroid genes' was much less than the proportion of African ancestry."

Race, my friends, is a social construct. Our obsession with mulattoes, quadroons, and octoroons has nothing to do with science, and everything to do with society.

I am not sure why people have gone to all this linguistic trouble over the years. Traditionally, if you were known to have any black ancestors, you were simply considered black. Just ask any person of any shade of blackness who tried to go to a white school, live in a white neighbourhood, argue with a white person, eat in a white restaurant, or excuse himself from slavery.

. . .

Discussions of who is black and who is white could fill countless books. One book that manages to be original, fascinating, and dismaying is the 863-page *Dictionary of Latin American Racial and Ethnic Terminology*. In it, Thomas Stephens, a Rutgers University professor, offers seven thousand racial and ethnic terms from Spanish, Portuguese, and American French Creole. Chew that notion over for a moment. *Seven thousand* terms. Here are some samples: the Spanish *negro humo*, meaning "a black person with smoke-black skin colour"; the Portuguese *quadrarao*, meaning a "person of one-quarter black ancestry"; and thanks to the imaginative French Creole, we have *malblanchi* (literally "badly whitened"), which refers to a "person of mixed race," and *marabou*, which defines a "person who is from forty to forty-eight parts white." Unfortunately, Professor Stephens did not venture to explain how the person who coined *marabou* managed to count the forty-eight white parts, or where, precisely, they are located in the anatomy. Conventional wisdom, however, would tell us that the remaining fifty-two to sixty parts are black, and that they can be found in the brain (said to be small), the genitals (well endowed, or so they say), the pigment (you pick the shade), and the lips (no collagen required).

Today, some people might hesitate to declare that the child of black and white parents is black. Why? Because we subscribe to what I will call the "paint mixture theory," an unexamined assumption that the child somehow represents an equal mixture of the two parents, and therefore is neither black nor white but somewhere in between. Grey, like the mixed paints.

This belief is as erroneous as it is pervasive. There is no biological difference between black people and white people. One cannot use genetics to explain race. And since black and white people can't be distinguished genetically, their children—whatever their mixtures—can't be grouped into neat genetic categories either.

One of the world's most renowned geneticists is Albert Jacquard of France. In the March 1996 edition of the *UNESCO Courier*, Jacquard noted that the concept of race is invalid for human beings. He wrote: "The reason why the concept is not valid is well known. If a genetic inheritance is to acquire a certain originality, if it is to distinguish itself significantly from that of neighbouring groups, it has to remain in complete isolation for a very long period, or for roughly as many generations as there are individuals of reproductive age. That kind of isolation can exist in the case of animals, but is barely conceivable for a species as nomadic and as keenly curious as ours. Because we are capable of crossing mountain ranges and oceans, we have homogenized our genetic inheritances.

"That observation can be illustrated by the following figures: the proportion of the total genetic diversity of the human species that can be put down to differences between the four traditional 'races' is only 7–8 per cent. In the case of differences between nations within these races, it is also only 7–8 per cent, while the remaining 85 per cent is due to differences between groups belonging to the same nation. In other words, the essential differences are not between groups, but contained within them. The concept of race consequently has so little content that the word becomes meaningless and should be eradicated from our vocabulary."

If "race" is in itself a meaningless term, then so is "mixed race." I have used the term "mixed race" all my life, but now see it as an utter absurdity, even as I use it in this book. For a spell, I contemplated using the expression "mixed ancestry" instead. But it seems imprecise. A person of Scottish and Welsh background could be said to be of mixed ancestry, but such a person is not of mixed race. For me, the key is to remember that race has no scientific meaning, and is nothing more than an arbitrary and fluid social convention.

The arbitrariness of race was brought home for me when I moved to Quebec in 1978 to finish an economics degree at Université Laval. Overnight, I went from being black to being an *anglais*. Nobody in any other place I had lived to that point in my life had ever seen me that way. In Quebec, however, my linguistic identity was more important than my racial background.

Several of my interviewees shared stories of their own experiences with the arbitrariness of race. One of the most fascinating came from Catherine Slaney, who grew up as a white girl in Toronto in the 1950s. Nobody told her that half of her ancestors were black. Why? Because her light-skinned grandparents chose to "pass" as white and did so with such success that even their own daughter—Catherine's mother—was kept in the dark about her family history. One day, my father wrote a feature article in a Toronto newspaper about Canada's first black doctor—a man named Anderson Ruffin Abbott. Catherine Slaney saw the article and was dumbfounded. She recognized the name of her great-grandfather, but nobody had ever told her he was black. Intrigued, she embarked on years of research to pin down her family story—not only the accomplishments of Anderson Ruffin Abbott, but the truth of how some of his descendants passed for white. After a long midlife journey, Catherine now sees herself sometimes as a person of colour and at other moments as a white woman with black ancestors. But the discovery altered forever how she saw herself, and even how others perceived her.

As the noted scholar Henry Louis Gates Jr. pointed out in *The New Yorker*, Anatole Paul Broyard was born black in 1920, raised in a coloured neighbourhood in the French Quarter of New Orleans, and moved into Greenwich Village in New York City at the end of the Second World War. When he moved to New York, Broyard decided to pass himself off as white in order to make it as "a writer, rather than a Negro writer." He became one of America's foremost book reviewers, for many years writing daily for the *New York Times*. Virtually everyone who interacted with him thought Broyard was a white man.

In no arena of Canadian life is racial identity more absurd—and more fluid—than in the context of Aboriginal peoples, defined in our 1982 Constitution as Indians, Inuit, and Metis. Some might argue that this classification has nothing to do with the black or the mixed-race experience. But my research led me to a conflict involving Aboriginal people that sheds much light on the absurdity of rigid racial categorization. By extension, it helps us shoot down any claim that definitions such as white, black, one-half black, and one-quarter black have any scientific validity.

Until 1985, when the federal *Indian Act* inched out of the Stone Age, any Indian woman (that is, any woman defined as such by the Act) lost her legal status as an Indian if she married a non-Indian. Any children of such a union had no status as Indians, either. And any non-Indian woman who married a status Indian legally became one, too. If the Queen of England had dumped her husband, moved to Churchill, Manitoba, and tied the knot with a status Indian, she, too, would have become one. To add insult to injury, until the *Canada Elections Act* was amended in 1960, status Indians could not vote in federal elections, or in provincial elections until that year or a little earlier, depending on the province.

This meant that any non-Indian woman who married an Indian lost the right to vote. Why? Because she had suddenly become an Indian, in the legal sense, and could no longer be trusted with such weighty responsibilities.

In February 2001, the Ontario Court of Appeal waded into the murky waters of Metis identity. Metis people, like the historic martyr Louis Riel, whose Red River Resistance led to the creation of the province of Manitoba in 1870, are people of mixed European and native ancestry.

The court ruled to acquit Steve Powley and his son, Roddy, of the charge of hunting moose without a licence. It accepted the Powleys' argument that they were members of the historic Metis community and therefore entitled, under the Canadian Constitution, to hunt without a licence.

The Crown fought for a conviction, using, as one of its grounds, the argument that Steve Powley was only $\frac{1}{64}$th Metis and that his son, Roddy, was only $\frac{1}{128}$th Metis.

Indeed, this issue was raised during the trial at the Ontario Court of Justice. The trial judge, Charles Vaillancourt, wrote in his ruling, "In the case at bar, Mr. Steve Powley has $\frac{1}{64}$ Aboriginal blood and his son, Roddy, has $\frac{1}{128}$. Should there be a minimum percentage to qualify a person to claim Metis status?" Thankfully, he appeared to answer his own question in the negative. "Without a universally accepted definition of Metis to be found, I shall attempt to distil a basic, workable definition of who is a Metis. Accordingly, I find that a Metis is a person of Aboriginal ancestry, who self identifies as a Metis, and who is accepted by the Metis community as a Metis."

The unfortunate aspect to this ruling is that the judge's very language of the ruling—"$\frac{1}{64}$ Aboriginal blood"—suggests that it is possible to quantify racial identity. I must say that I find it hard to imagine any person using a definition such as ¹⁄₆₄th or ¹⁄₁₂₈th Metis with a straight face. Thankfully, however, Judge Vaillancourt ruled that the Powleys were indeed Metis, and his decision was upheld on two appeals within the Ontario courts.

. . .

So what on earth *is* a black person? A person whose ancestors are from Africa? That hardly works—the human species originated in Africa. We're all Africans if you go back far enough. And what, for that matter, is a white person?

One common synonym for white is the term "Caucasian," coined by the eighteenth-century physician and anthropologist Johann Friedrich Blumenbach. If Blumenbach's intention was to confound future generations about the precise meaning of "white" or "Caucasian," and to send scientists in the wrong direction for the better part of two hundred years, the good doctor couldn't have done a better job. Blumenbach influenced language for centuries to come, both by coining the term "race" and by arbitrarily dividing humans into five racial categories: Caucasian, Mongolian, Ethiopian, American, and Malay.

Check out the first of those five categories, named after the inhabitants of the Caucasus Mountains, in Russia. Blumenbach's personal biases speak for themselves. This is how he sang the praises of his newly dubbed Caucasian race: "I have taken the name from Mount Caucasus because it produces the most beautiful race of men. I have not observed a single ugly face in that country in either sex. Nature has lavished upon the women beauties which are not seen elsewhere. I consider it impossible to look at them without loving them."

But it turns out that the Caucasus Mountains form part of

a geological range that sweeps across Europe, northern India, the Middle East, and North Africa. That allows a whole lotta people to walk around calling themselves Caucasian. The on-line version of *Merriam-Webster's Collegiate Dictionary* defines "Caucasian" as (1) of or relating to the Caucasus or its inhabitants, (2)(a) of or relating to the white race of humankind as classified according to physical features, and (b) of or relating to the white race as defined by law specifically as composed of persons of European, North African, or southwest Asian ancestry.

This trick of geography was not lost upon Bhagat Tingh Thind of India, who in 1923 asked the United States Supreme Court to rule that he was indeed a Caucasian, and therefore a white person, and therefore eligible for American citizenship. Thind, who was a high-caste Hindu born in Amritsar, had been granted a certificate of American citizenship, but the certificate was soon cancelled "on the ground that the appellee was not a white person and therefore not lawfully entitled to naturalization."

As Donald Braman noted in "Of Race and Immutability," an article in the June 1999 edition of the *UCLA Law Review*, "The argument presented in *Thind* hinged on the appellant's claim that, as an 'Aryan Hindu,' Thind was a member of the Caucasian race and thus a white person . . ."

The court, however, shot the poor man down. Justice Sutherland, who wrote the opinion, had this to say: "It may be true that the blond Scandinavian and the brown Hindu have a common ancestor in the dim reaches of antiquity, but the average man knows perfectly well that there are unmistakable and profound differences between them today."

A few paragraphs later, Sutherland went on to hint at the social impossibility of Americans accepting that Thind was white, or Caucasian. According to some, Sutherland wrote, the Caucasian race "includes not only the Hindu, but some of the Polynesians (that is, the Maori, Tahitians, Samoans, Hawaiians, and others), the Hamites of Africa, upon the ground of the Caucasic cast of their features, though in color they range from brown to black. We venture to think that the average well-informed white American would learn with some degree of astonishment that the race to which he belongs is made up of such heterogeneous elements."

The United States Supreme Court was unequivocal in telling Bhagat Tingh Thind, *Good try, but goodbye.* But let's give Bhagat Tingh Thind his due for shedding light on the foibles of our very language. The next time you hear someone use the word "Caucasian," try this as a comeback: "You mean people from India, right?"

. . .

In a North American context, the terms "black" and "white" ultimately acquire meaning only in opposition to each other. A white is somebody who is not black, Asian, or Aboriginal. A black is someone who is not white. Up until this last generation or so, when the lines have become more blurred, you were black if you were known to have any black ancestors. And you were white if nobody could prove that you were black.

Consider how the Canadian government instructed its enumerators in the 1901 Census. For this, the Fourth Census of Canada, the document *Instructions to Officers* ran to ninety-seven paragraphs and included this gem: "The races of men will be designated by the use of W for white, R for red, B for black and Y for yellow. The whites are, of course, the Caucasian race, the reds are the American Indian, the blacks are the African or Negro, and the yellow are the Mongolian (Japanese and Chinese). But only pure whites will be classed as whites; the children begotten of marriages between whites and any one of the other races will be classed as red, black or yellow, as the case may be, irrespective of the degree of colour."

This is the famous "one-drop rule." If you have one drop of black blood, or so the North American saying goes, you're black. This rule was applied vigorously and viciously in the United States, but the instruction to census enumerators is a Canadian pearl indeed—one of the truly rare examples of Canadian authorities wading in to define just exactly what a black person is.

From what I've been able to gather, nine decades would pass before Canadian authorities would again attempt to define black people. This time, it was done in the name of social justice. In the early 1990s, under Premier Bob Rae, the Ontario government introduced the *Employment Equity Act*, which sought to improve employment opportunities for groups judged to have been traditionally disadvantaged: women, people with disabilities, Aboriginal people, and racial minorities. And just how would a person qualify to be considered, say, black? Self-definition.

And in the year 2000, a full century after Canadian census-takers were informed that any child of one black parent would be deemed black as well, the Nova Scotia government became what was likely the first elected body in this country to advance a specific definition of black people. Again, the intent was to promote social justice.

That year, after pressure from some black community leaders, the provincial government took legal steps to ensure that at least one black person would be elected to each regional and district school board in the province. Under the amended *Education Act*, there is now to be a black representative on each school board—and only

"African Nova Scotian electors" are entitled to vote for them. If you want to vote for an African Nova Scotian school board representative, you have to sign a form at the ballot box indicating that you yourself are an African Nova Scotian elector. Again, self-definition.

I dug around to find out just exactly how one would define an African Nova Scotian elector. The answer lies right on Form 43, which you sign at the ballot box if you're voting for an African Nova Scotian representative. It says, "Under the *Education Act*, an 'African Nova Scotian elector' is defined to mean a person who is qualified to vote in an election of a school board AND (a) who is an African Nova Scotian or a black person, OR (b) who is the parent of an African Nova Scotian or a black person."

Self-definition is emerging as a key way to define one's identity. In speaking with Mike Sweeney, a senior official with the Nova Scotia Department of Education, I noted that the government had basically concluded a black person was any person who calls himself or herself a black person, and I asked whether anyone had considered advancing a more specific definition of blackness. "We weren't going to go down that road," he said wryly.

So at the outset of the twenty-first century, how are people of dual ancestry to see themselves, to develop a sense of identity, and to situate themselves in society? Some are insulted to be called "mixed." They are black, and that is that. Some people prefer the term "brown." That word has always irritated me, especially when it comes from the white community, because it trivializes the black experience in North America. It suggests that race is nothing more than the colour of a person's skin. According to that way of thinking, black people of light hue would be more accurately described as brown. But this seems to me to negate the rigid social categories into which black people have traditionally been thrust regardless of their skin tone.

Let's not lose sight of our own history. Just fifty years ago, thirty U.S. states still forbade marriages between whites and blacks. Violations were often punishable by fine or imprisonment. Americans were still busy enforcing segregation in schools, public accommodations, restaurants, and housing. In some states, militias, boxing matches, and fraternal organizations had to be segregated. Oklahoma required separate telephone booths for blacks and whites. Can you imagine the nervous breakdowns that the Oklahoma authorities would have suffered if e-mail had existed back then? What if they had had to police chat rooms? And before we get too high and mighty about our moral superiority north of the forty-ninth parallel, let's remember a few facts: slavery existed in Canada until its abolition in 1834; the federal government did its level best to prevent U.S. blacks from immigrating to the Canadian prairies in the early 1900s; we allowed black Canadian soldiers to give up their lives in the First and Second World Wars but wouldn't let them sleep in hotels, eat in restaurants, skate on public ice rinks, or apply for most jobs; the Ontario legislature permitted school segregation until 1964. And don't forget that tomorrow or the next day a few dozen young black men across the country will be stopped by police simply for driving Jaguars or BMWs. When you think of all these people who have been—and will be—subjected to such indignities, tell me this: Were they brown?

Of the thirty or so interviews I conducted with people of mixed race, I heard the most succinct comment about self-definition from Sara, the anonymous subject from London. "I didn't decide I was black," Sara told me. "It was decided for me. I was identified, labelled, categorized as that. I had to learn to get comfortable within that label. I certainly wasn't as a youngster, nor as a late teen. I rejected that label. I rejected it because everything that came with that label in my environment was negative. My only positive black experiences, so to speak, were at my own family table, my homecoming, going to my grandmother's, my cousins. So I had to learn how to be comfortable within that title, embrace it and identify with it. And that's how I identify myself."

I Was Here
Before the Klan!

All the research I did on the arbitrariness of race and the importance of self-definition brought to mind an incident I fictionalized in my novel *Any Known Blood*. I now have some misgivings about the scene, and they stem from an encounter I had in 1997, while on a cross-country tour to promote the book.

After a reading, I was approached by a white bookstore manager, who clasped my hand, took a minute to wax enthusiastic about the novel, and then said, "You know what I really love about this novel? And do you know one of the reasons why it's going to sell? When I read your book, I didn't have to feel guilty for being white."

My instinctive reaction was to remind her that a number of ugly things happened to black people in the book: slavery, torture, and housing discrimination, to name a few. In the very first scene, lovemaking between a black man and a white woman is interrupted when racists hurl a rock through their window.

"Yes, yes, I know all that," the bookstore manager said. "But the way you wrote it . . . well, I didn't have to feel bad for being a white person."

I'm not interested, as a writer, in making anybody feel guilt for anything. Wallowing in a generalized bad feeling about oneself—or about one's race—is hardly useful, and it can actually inhibit concrete action. However, I don't like to think that something I wrote absolved the reader of a sense of social responsibility. On the contrary, I want my readers to see my scenes, to live them, and possibly to learn from them. Perhaps for that reason, the conversation with the bookstore manager slid under my skin and stayed there. I could not forget her words: "I didn't have to feel guilty for being white." Had I made a misstep? When he taught me creative writing at Johns Hopkins University, the American novelist John Barth used to say that readers were mischievous creatures, and that one of the challenges of narrative was to keep them from wandering off to places where they had no business. Had I given the bookstore manager too much room to wander? Had I let her get into mischief? Had I allowed her to think that she didn't have to consider her own life in a society that still oppresses black people?

In the few years that have passed since that encounter, I have come to the conclusion that one key scene in the novel might have made it easier for the bookstore manager to let herself off the hook. The scene in question described the Ku Klux Klan raiding Oakville in 1930. In reality, the KKK did come to Oakville on February 28, 1930, to split up a black man named Ira Johnson and a white woman named Isabella Jones. The two were living as a couple at the time and planning to get married.

In the novel, the Klansmen drive into Oakville one wintry day, congregate outside the house where the couple is staying, make a lot of threatening noises, hurl rocks through the windows, try in vain to set up a cross on the front lawn, and throw a burning torch at the house. They scare the hell out of their intended targets, but they are confronted and held off by the black church minister, in whose house the couple is hiding. And then they are easily derailed when an irate woman—the older sister of the black man who is their target—shows up and begins to excoriate the Klansmen. The Klansmen look like buffoons and disintegrate into chaos. When the local police chief arrives and arrests the Klansmen, the scene ends. We learn later that the black man does marry the white woman, on the Six Nations reserve in Brantford, Ontario. So what the reader gets is a scene where the Klansmen, although at first truly frightening, are soon made to look like idiots (which is fair enough) and put in their place. Was this scene sufficiently candy-coated to allow the bookstore manager to feel that the Klan's raid was an entertaining but insignificant part of Oakville's history? I'm afraid it was. Particularly given what really happened.

· · ·

On the night of February 28, 1930, when seventy-five hooded Klansmen drove from Hamilton to Oakville to prevent him from marrying a twenty-year-old white woman, Ira Johnson was thirty-six years old. He had been born and raised in the black community in Oakville. Ira's mother, Ida Johnson, worked as a midwife. She delivered Alvin Duncan, who today is an eighty-seven-year-old black man from Oakville and the source of some of my information about the Johnson family. Alvin explained that up until the KKK raid, the Johnsons were considered important members of Oakville's black community.

Ira Johnson was born in Oakville on April 30, 1893. Early in the 1900s, the local tannery was a mainstay of employment in Oakville, and it's not surprising to discover from

Ira's First World War military records that he worked as a tanner before enlisting for war service on March 16, 1916. Ira's Attestation Paper for the 164th Battalion, Canadian Overseas Expeditionary Force, indicates that he had already done two months of military service with the 20th Halton Rifles. It gives his height as five feet, eight inches, his chest "girth, when fully expanded" as thirty-four and a half inches, his complexion, eyes, and hair each as "dark," and his religious denomination as Methodist. It also notes that he previously had gonorrhea.

Ira Johnson served as a private during the First World War and saw active duty in France. His wartime service must have been painful. He was treated for one bout of tonsillitis and three bouts of gonorrhea. He spent sixty-nine days in army hospitals after losing his footing on a muddy, frosted ladder, falling twenty feet and sustaining a "serious" fracture to his left leg. Then, on September 18, 1918, at Vimy Ridge in France, shrapnel shattered Ira's right tibia. He had to wait two weeks for surgery to remove the metal from his leg. The procedure left him with a long scar along the inner edge of his shin. He was later deemed "medically unfit," shipped home to Canada, and discharged in Hamilton on July 2, 1919. For his efforts overseas, he received one good conduct stripe as well as British war and victory medals.

After the war, Ira returned to Oakville. Alvin Duncan recalls that Ira Johnson, like his father, played the accordion. "Everybody liked Ira. He was an easygoing chap." He worked for five years as a motor mechanic and later did odd jobs in town. Ira eventually met Isabella Jones, the daughter of Annie Jones, who was one of Ida Johnson's white co-workers at the Salvation Army. They began dating, but when they grew more involved and began spending a number of nights together, Annie Jones became frantic.

In her desperation, Annie Jones contacted Oakville's police chief, David Kerr, the town magistrate, W.E. McIlveen, and a Captain Broome of the local Salvation Army, but all of them told her they were powerless to separate her white daughter and the black man. On March 3, 1930, the *Globe and Mail* quoted McIlveen as saying, "She [Annie Jones] asked me to help her in getting her daughter away from Johnson, after it had been discovered that she was living with him." But McIlveen declared that he had no power to interfere as her daughter was over eighteen.

Finally, Annie Jones contacted the Ku Klux Klan. In a written statement made public shortly after the raid, the Klan acknowledged that it had kept Ira Johnson and Isabella Jones under surveillance for several days. When the couple went on February 28, 1930, to obtain a marriage licence, the Klan swung into high gear. That same night, seventy-five hooded Klansmen assembled in Hamilton and drove in a procession to Oakville.

First, the men gathered on Kerr Street, just west of the centre of town, planted a cross with oil-soaked rags in the middle of the street, set it ablaze, and stood quietly watching while the timber burned. Alvin Duncan, who was on his way to meet his mother at a function at the black church, says he saw the hooded Klansmen. "Everybody who was black knew of the Ku Klux Klan," he said. "I couldn't believe my eyes to think that they were the KKK."

After setting fire to the cross, the mob of hooded men went to the local police station to tell Chief Kerr about their business in town. It was evening, however, and Kerr wasn't in. Alvin Duncan speculates to this day that the police chief may have been a Klansman himself. "There was some doubt in the black community about which side Chief Kerr was on," Duncan said.

The Klansmen then moved to a house on Head Street where they knew that Ira Johnson and Isabella Jones had been staying. But Ira and Isabella were out playing cards in the home of Isabella's aunt on nearby Kerr Street, so the Klansmen went there.

In *Colour-Coded: A Legal History of Racism in Canada, 1900–1950*, Constance Backhouse, a law professor at the University of Ottawa, described what happened next: "According to the *Hamilton Spectator*, the KKK members 'thundered on the door and demanded of the negro who answered them that he bring out [the] white girl.' Twenty-year-old Isabel [sic] Jones emerged, and was hustled off to the home of her white, widowed mother. After a brief consultation with Mrs. Jones, Isabel [sic] was put into a car and deposited in the care of Captain W. Broome, a white officer of the Salvation Army.

"The Klansmen then returned for Ira Johnson and forcibly removed the terrified man, casting him into another car with 'two stalwarts' as guards on either side. The caravan collected Ira Johnson's elderly aunt and uncle from their home, and drove back to Head Street. The costumed marauders surrounded the house, and turned Ira Johnson and his relatives out in the front yard. Then they nailed a large cross to a post in front of the door and set it on fire. They threatened that, if Ira Johnson was 'ever seen walking down the street with a white girl again,' the Klan 'would attend to him.'

"Meanwhile, one of Oakville's Black citizens [the local track athlete and baseball player Ollie Johnson, whom Alvin Duncan says was related to Ira Johnson] had located the police chief and alerted him to the situation. Chief Kerr headed out to investigate, and came upon a cavalcade of 15 cars on Navy Street, all filled with white-robed men. When the chief caught up with the leaders of the procession, several of the gowned men got out and took off their hoods. Chief Kerr recognized them as white residents of the nearby city of Hamilton, whom he 'knew quite well.' They all shook hands. The police chief assured himself that 'no damage to property or person warranting his interference' had occurred. Kerr made no arrests, offered no warnings or further complaint, and the Klansmen continued on their way."

The most astonishing part of the Oakville KKK incident was its aftermath. It was left to black and Jewish community leaders in Toronto to express their outrage over the event, and to demand that W.H. Price, attorney general of Ontario, have the incident investigated and charges laid. Community leaders in Oakville expressed nothing but a smug indulgence for the KKK, and a general satisfaction that justice had been served on the night that Isabella Jones was pried from the arms of a black man.

In the days following the incident, most papers in Oakville and the surrounding region reported favourably on the KKK's activities. As the front page story in the *Globe* on March 1 stated, "There was not the semblance of disorder and the visitors' behaviour was all that could be desired, according to Chief David Kerr of the Oakville Police Department, who did not interfere with the demonstrators."

On March 4, the *Toronto Daily Star* quoted Kerr to the same effect: "They [the Klansmen] destroyed no property and harmed no one. It was just one of those unusual incidents that occasionally crops up."

On March 1, the *Star* quoted Oakville mayor J.B. Moat:

"There was a strong feeling against the marriage which the young girl and the negro had planned . . . Personally I think the Ku Klux Klan acted quite properly in the matter. The feeling in the town is generally against such a marriage. It will be quite an object lesson."

On March 7, the *Oakville Star* seemed positively gleeful about the KKK raid. "Certainly this old town wakened up last Saturday morning when it became known that on the previous evening a squad of Ku Klux Klan had visited Oakville, and, for the first time in Canada, had exercised one of their chief objectives," the paper reported. "That was to discourage and, if possible, prevent the marriage of a colored man and a white girl. The action was taken as the result of an appeal made to the Klan by the girl's mother. It was really impressive how thoroughly and how systematically the Klan went about the task."

On March 5, the *Toronto Daily Star* quoted Toronto lawyer A.B. Hassard: ". . . From what I have read, my sympathies are strongly with the girl and her mother, but unfortunately the law is the other way. If this practice of intermarrying whites and negroes be extensively carried on some society ought to secure the enactment of a uniform law throughout Canada on the subject. If the Klansmen are really in earnest they would be the proper people to do that.

"There is no law against whites and blacks intermarrying, but I think there should be. I think that neither the marriage license issuer nor a minister who has any respect for himself would, except under the gravest condition, assist in the marriage of a white and a black. The same should be said of the marriage of a white girl and a Chinese."

B.J. Spencer Pitt, a black lawyer from Toronto, helped push for charges to be laid after the incident. But that didn't mean that he condoned the idea of interracial relationships.

He told the *Star*, "If the Canadian government saw fit to prohibit intermarriage of Negroes and whites, I am certain that we Negroes would abide by the law."

Very few people stood up for the right of Ira Johnson and Isabella Jones to come together as a couple. Even Alvin Duncan, who had celebrated his sixteenth birthday one day before the Ku Klux Klan came to Oakville, was not pleased with the news that Ira Johnson had taken up with a white woman. "I thought that he was a Negro and that he should associate with Negroes," Alvin told me in an interview. "He was sort of stepping on dangerous ground." At the time, Alvin knew that the Klan had a long history of torturing and murdering black people in the United States, and that it was active in Canada. He felt that by consorting with a white woman, Ira Johnson was putting himself and others in harm's way, and getting too big for his britches. "Lynchings were common in the United States. It was common for blacks to be strung up from trees. Oakville is only a two-hour ride from the border. We were worried that there may have been a first lynching here in Oakville."

As Backhouse points out, E. Lionel Cross, a black lawyer in Toronto, was the most vocal critic of Oakville's smug acceptance of the KKK raid. On March 1, the *London Free Press* quoted him as saying, "I call the doings at Oakville last evening an outrage. As a British citizen, I have believed the rule of law should always prevail. [A man] is free to choose what companions he cares to have. When anybody under the guise of patriotism or any other 'ism' trespasses on the right of any man, no matter who he may be or of what race, it should be the duty of all law abiding citizens to denounce any such action."

It is worth noting the widespread support at the time for the KKK's raid on Oakville, but to my eye, the most significant part of the story has escaped public attention. Four short days after the Klansmen warned him that they'd harm him if he ever walked down the street again with a white woman, Johnson dropped a bombshell. He told the *Toronto Daily Star* that he was in fact an Indian, and that he had not an ounce of Negro blood in his veins.

The media, which had been crawling all over Oakville and cranking out front page stories across Ontario, scrambled to make sense of the news. The *Star* put itself through absurdly comic contortions in order to roll with Ira Johnson's story. On the front page on March 5, 1930, the paper reported this story:

IS OF INDIAN DESCENT
IRA JOHNSTON [*sic*] INSISTS
Oakville Man, Separated from
Sweetheart, Traces His
Ancestry
OF CHEROKEE ORIGIN
Maternal Grandfather a White
Minister, Who Preached to
Colored Congregation
Oakville, March 5—Ira Junius Johnston, separated from his sweetheart, Alice [sic] Jones by Ku Klux Klansmen here last Friday, is of Indian descent and has not a drop of negro blood in his veins, he told The Star today at the home of his mother, who is a refined and intelligent woman.

Johnston's maternal grandfather was Rev. Junius Roberts, white, who preached for many years to negro congregations in Ontario, having had charges at Guelph, Hamilton and Oakville more than 40 years ago. He was at Oakville for about three years until his health failed and he went to Detroit, where he died . . . Ira's maternal grandmother was a Cherokee Indian and his maternal grandfather of Scottish and English parents.

Ira Johnston says that the reason his grandfather preached in the church for negroes was because Mrs. Roberts was so dark that some objections had been taken to her by members of white congregations.

In talking to The Star, Johnston had a straight account of his forebears in Indiana and Maryland. His contention that there is not a drop of negro blood in his veins appears to be quite clear.

He is quiet and unassuming in his demeanor and his features reveal his Indian connection. His hair is black and straight. As to where the Ku Klux Klan got the idea that he was a negro, he says he has no idea and is inclined to think that "the joke is on them."

The next day, the *Star* outdid itself by running photos of Ira Johnson, Isabella Jones, and eight of Ira's relatives. Under the photos ran the main cutline: "Johnson Family Tree Shows Indian, Scotch, Irish and Spanish Descent—No African Strain." The rest of the detailed caption provided the racial or ethnic backgrounds of Ira Johnson's ancestors, from his father to his paternal grandparents on one side of the family, and from his mother to his maternal great-grandparents on the other side. The descriptions came solely from Ira Johnson.

If you ask me, Ira Johnson proved himself as Canada's first spin doctor. Never mind the fact that Johnson had lived his first thirty-six years as a black man in Oakville. Never mind that he had socialized with the black community, that his mother was a midwife who delivered black babies, that two of his relatives had pastored at the African

Methodist Episcopal Church in town, that he had taken part in local minstrel shows that featured blacks, that he was related to the local athlete Ollie Johnson, or that Ira himself, his parents, and his sisters were listed as being "black" and of "African" ethnic origin in the 1901 Canada Census— never mind all that.

The minute Ira Johnson stood up and declared that he was Cherokee and not black, the media acquiesced and said, "Okay, if you say so." No one examined census records. No one conducted detailed interviews with members of Oakville's black community. No one thoughtfully or carefully examined the facts, or the possibility that Ira Johnson may have had both black and Indian ancestry—something that is common among North American blacks.

My father howled with laughter when I first told him the story of Ira Johnson and his revelations. "Did he think that would save his ass? That the Klan would look any more favourably on his being an Indian, than a black man, if he were going to be taking a good white girl into his bed?"

Johnson's midlife transition from black to Indian speaks volumes about the entirely sociological manner in which race has come to be defined. In the chaos and fear of the days after the raid, whether to save his own bacon or for some other reason, Johnson became the first Canadian I know of who stood up and essentially said, *Hey, folks, you've got me all wrong. You thought I was coloured, but I'm not. I don't have a drop of Negro blood in my veins.* This behaviour is disturbing because it illustrates the arbitrariness of our attempts to define people according to race. It makes clear the fact that we have built an entire house of social classification—racial identity—on Styrofoam studs.

Johnson's story demonstrates that race is nothing but a social construction. Your race is determined by how you see yourself, and how society sees you. We have functioned this way in North America for four hundred years, although we haven't fully owned up to it. Instead, we have maintained the fiction that race is a matter of genetics and arithmetic proportions. Yet when Ira Johnson stood up and told the world that he wasn't black, nobody mounted a genetic argument to the contrary because there was no such argument to mount. And nobody could build a sociological argument— the "one drop" rule, which was the only real argument available—because nobody in the Toronto media that covered the event knew his family. If somebody had found out about his family, they might have been able to challenge his identity. But Canadians, being Canadians, simply tossed up their hands and said, *Whatever. You're Indian? Then so be it.* The real genius of Ira Johnson's bombshell wasn't that he said he wasn't black. It was that he gave Canadians something else to hang onto: a Cherokee heritage. He traded one despised minority identity for another.

Ira Johnson could have cooked up the story entirely or partially, or the story could be entirely true. We may never know his precise ancestry. It hardly matters now. Most significant to me is that the Klan came to Oakville, that many of the townspeople welcomed it with open arms, and that Ira Johnson successfully transformed his own racial identity by means of one interview with the *Toronto Daily Star*.

What became of the incident? In the end, only one of the Klansmen—the ringleader, a Hamilton chiropractor by the name of William A. Phillips—was punished for the raid on Oakville. Phillips was initially convicted of wearing a mask by night and fined fifty dollars. Silly man. He appealed his conviction to the Ontario Court of Appeal, which ruled against him and increased the punishment to a three-month jail sentence.

And what became of the happy couple? Ira Johnson and Isabella Jones stayed apart for a few days after the KKK raid, but they reunited shortly thereafter and decided to get married after all. However, the minister of Oakville's African Methodist Episcopal Church, who had initially planned to marry them, wanted nothing to do with the couple after the KKK visit. The Salvation Army, to which Ira's and Isabella's mothers both belonged, wouldn't marry them, either. The local church ministers were clearly spooked, and perhaps for good reason. On March 18, the house in which Ira Johnson had been living before the raid was burned to the ground. The house and its contents were destroyed.

Four days later, Ira Johnson and Isabella Jones were married by Rev. Frank Burgess, a white pastor of the United Church, on the New Credit reserve near Brantford, Ontario. In January 2001, I had the chance to speak to Neil Burgess, the son of Rev. Frank Burgess. Neil Burgess, a retired United Church minister who was eighty-five years old at the time of the interview, was present when his father married the couple in 1930: "My mother [Olive May Size] implored my father not to get involved with this at all because it might be a personal danger to the family, and Father made his famous pronouncement [quoted in the *Toronto Star*], 'I was here before the Klan.'"

I asked Neil if he had been frightened by the possibility of violence, given the KKK's interest in the matter. And he answered, "For the next couple of weeks, I wore a softball bat under my trouser leg, suspended from my belt, just in case I needed it." Just for the record, I also asked Neil Burgess how his father had perceived the races of the couple from Oakville. "Father's perception," he told me, "would be that Ira Johnson was black. That had been his firm conviction—that he had married a black man and a white girl."

Ira Johnson and Isabella Jones soon faded from the public spotlight. They remained in Oakville and had two children. Ira worked for many years as a gardener on the estate of Major W.F. Eaton, and later served as a school crossing guard. After being a patient for two months at the Oakville-Trafalgar Memorial Hospital, Ira Johnson died at age seventy-three, on December 23, 1966.

In the end, what can we make of Ira Johnson's ancestry? As usual, race was only an issue when Canadians made it one, and in his most difficult hour, when the pressure was ballooning all around him, Ira Johnson with one deft pin-prick made all the hot air dissipate by simply, cleverly, and irrevocably trading one racial identity for another.

Conclusion:
Say It Ain't So

Canadians are quick to point out what we of mixed race are not—we are not white, and we are not black—but they don't tell us what we are.

This is the quintessential Canada: the True North, Proud, and Vague.

What interests me is that, in recent years, it has become possible to define oneself on one's own terms. That people are debating the matter at all is a very recent phenomenon in North American society. Is a child of mixed race to be considered biracial, with polite nods in the directions of both parents? Or is this child free to call himself or herself black and live accordingly?

When I was a boy, I suppose that I could have walked around telling people, "I'm not black. I've got one black parent and one white parent, and I consider myself biracial, and that's just who I am." And that strategy might have worked for the most part, although any person who felt negatively disposed toward black people would hardly have been kinder to me as a result of this self-definition.

I had no desire to make such a statement, however. I didn't think of myself as both black and white. When I thought about my racial identity—and naturally, some periods of time passed when I didn't think about it at all—I generally considered myself black. And I felt frustrated by the knowledge that at the same time, my own cousins—some as light-skinned as I was—were attending segregated schools in North Carolina. I had been down to visit them, and they sure as hell weren't viewed as anything except black.

Growing up, I was aware that Canada provided me with a little manoeuvring space that my American cousins did not have. For example, I didn't have the weight of a legally sanctioned United States school system telling me that I had to attend this particular school because I was black. Unlike my cousins, I had at least some room to concoct my own identity, declare it, test it out, see how it flew out there in my world. This, I think, is what still defines Canada today for a mixed-race person. There is some wiggle room.

But, brothers and sisters, be warned. Canadians may let you wiggle occasionally, but you're going to have to scratch and claw like mad to get anywhere discernibly new.

Earlier in this book, I suggested that many light-skinned blacks, and mixed-race blacks such as myself, feel they must prove their blackness by asserting themselves through public involvement with the black community. That approach works fine for people like me. As I'm a writer, I am often invited into black communities to lecture or to read. I have opportunities to involve myself in black culture. Through my work, I have found it increasingly easy to feel engaged.

But what about people who have no public profile or who are naturally shy? What about people who don't work, or don't have work that makes them appear valuable in the eyes of the middle-class black community? People who long to feel connected to and accepted by the black community—and believe me, this feeling can be just as strong and rooted as the desire to bring a child into the world—but who have no means at their disposal to gain entry?

My sister, Karen Hill, experienced many of these feelings, especially when she was a teenager and a young adult in Canada. She definitely identified as black, longed to be more "darkly complected" (as some in my family like to say), and felt the sting of rejection by the black community for not being black enough. Was the rejection real? Was it partly imagined? It hardly matters. The rejection became her own emotional baggage, and it affected her view of herself as a young woman.

Unlike Dan and I, who found our identity through our work, Karen "became black"—or solidified her attachment to black culture—by forming friendships with black people, going out to black clubs, dating black men, and having a black child. But it hasn't been easy.

"Even though I may think of myself as black," she told me, "nobody else does. I just feel, somehow, that I don't fit in, that there's some sort of animosity over the whole skin colour thing. Obviously, intrinsically, I'm privileged [by virtue of having light skin]. I don't walk into stores and get followed around like some black people do. I consider myself black, but I haven't suffered the humiliations that some darker-skinned people have known."

This is the astounding bind that we light-skinned, mixed-race blacks sometimes find ourselves in. On the one hand, we have a tendency to strive for acceptance as members of the black community, but on the other, we constantly remind ourselves that we don't quite qualify because we haven't had it as bad as people who are much more visibly black.

But believing this idea makes no more sense than believing that you have to earn entry into the human family by virtue of your appearance, experiences, or actions. You're a human being because ... well, because you just are one. You get the automatic, lifelong, irrevocable membership card when you are born. You are no less or no more valuable to the human race because you live in poverty or have won the Nobel Prize, or because someone else thinks you are ugly or beautiful.

We black folks have been sundered and pitted against one another since we were tossed in chains on North American shores four centuries ago. It didn't help that our ancestors were raped with impunity, wrenched from their families, and split according to skin colour. The blackest of us—the ones with the least humanity in the eyes of slave owners—worked as field slaves. Some of the lightest of us got to work in the houses, where life was easier—if you consider rape to be softer on body and soul than the whip. Since we were ranked and classified and valued and set to work according to our skin colour, and since this gross violation of our humanity went on for two or three centuries, what could be more normal than for black people to have internalized some of these beliefs?

My sister's skin colour is not a situation of her own making. She didn't get to fill out a colour preference chart in the womb, selecting café au lait as her shade of choice. My sister and I are black simply because we are. We have black ancestry, and we identify with it, and that, dear friends, is that.

Skin colour? Out the window. From the time that we've been on this continent, the one-drop rule has applied. Race isn't about skin colour. It's about social categorization.

Political affiliation and community activism? Fine, if you like that sort of thing. Don't try to tell me, however, that you're black if you vote and militate against the established order, but less black if you like the world the way it is. If that were the case, you might have people changing their race on several occasions during their life!

The number of times you've been insulted or put down as a result of your race? I wouldn't wish a put-down or an insult on any person. It's not a competition. Perhaps this isn't a bad moment to remember one of the most famous lines by the English poet John Donne: "No man is an island, entire of itself . . ."

The point is that every incident of racism diminishes us all. It diminishes the racist, the target of the attack, and all of us in the human family, regardless of our race. If our neighbour has been attacked, then so have we.

My sister and I are many things. Human beings. Son and daughter. Parents. Canadians. Writers. Decent cooks, if I do say so myself. We also happen to be black. Because we say we are. Because we identify with this part of our ancestry. Who's going to say it ain't so?

• • •

I understand the hurt and the anger of the black woman who sees limited choices for herself and sees black men running off with white women.

I know that some people of mixed race have been put through the mill, dissed by their own racist parents and families, and taught to hate themselves. I see that establishing a sense of personal and racial identity when you have a black and a white parent can involve much ambiguity.

Ultimately, however, the struggle to find yourself, define yourself, carve out a sense of who you want to be in this world is a good one. It is a process that many human beings have to go through, for many reasons. Although the struggles that mixed-race people face are not well known or appreciated by most Canadians, that will change. We can make sure of it.

In the meantime, I get to go on living and breathing and acting out my life, occasionally thinking of race and placing myself in the context of black communities, and occasionally having the luxury—it should be a right, but sadly, it remains a luxury—of not thinking about it at all.

When my daughter throws her arms around my neck with love, I'm not stopping to ask myself if she loves me more or less because of my skin tone. When I soak up her love and return it, I am not clouding that love with thoughts of my own racial background.

I believe that we can do two things about people who fixate on our race and try to put us down as a result. We can fight them when the time is right and the fighting promises rewards. And we can grow in our own skins and in our own humanity.

Tiger Woods, the world's most famous golfer, likes to call himself a Cablinasian—in celebration of his Caucasian, black, and Asian ancestries. He can pull it off, of course, because he is Tiger Woods. Some time ago, if a young person with Tiger Woods's ancestry and skin colour had told the wrong person, "I am a Cablinasian," the answer may have come back, "Shut your mouth, boy, and get up on that slave block. I'm fixing to sell you for two thousand dollars."

Nonetheless, there is a certain wisdom and worldliness to Woods's position. He is making people think. He is challenging them. Do we have to embrace the idiotic and racist legacy of our past in North America? Or can we say, "Wait. Hold on. I have some rights here, and I'm going to assert them. One of my rights is to think of myself as I please. If you don't like it, to hell with you."

Cablinasian. I like it, but it's not for me. I am black. I am a lot more than just that, of course, but if you're pinning me down or if the police clubs start swinging or if three African-Canadian children are beaten up on their way to school, then yes, I am in touch with my ancestry, I know where I came from, and in that moment I am black. This is what I choose to be. Take it or leave it.

• • •

One cold November evening in 2000, I lined up a babysitter for my three children, made sure all was under control, and drove to Hamilton to interview a man for this book. Stefan Dubowski, twenty-six, was visibly black. He had brown skin and wore his tightly curled hair in dreadlocks. But it was clear in the first words of the interview that Stefan was uncomfortable with any discussion of race or his own racial identity.

He insisted that race "doesn't matter," and that it has never been a factor in his life. Racial matters were never discussed in his family home, he said—not even the reaction of his white father's family to the news that he was going to marry a black woman. When I asked if he had ever been to a function in the black community, Stefan shifted in his chair and said, "No, but I've never been to a white community function, either."

Stefan did acknowledge that his mother would be despondent to hear him deny the importance of race. When he was in his early teens, she had tried to warn him that he was at a disadvantage. "She told me that I had one strike against me, in terms of how other people saw me, because I wasn't white. That comment made me want to prove her wrong, to prove that I didn't have any strikes against me because I was of a different colour. I didn't believe that my mother's take on society was right. Her concepts, to me, were just so much paranoia." Stefan said that the comment upset him a great deal, and that he has spent much of his life trying to prove that race isn't a factor in his life.

I felt for Stefan as he avoided my questions and repeated that race didn't and shouldn't make a difference. He was clearly uncomfortable, and I found myself wondering if anything about our interview would lead him to examine his own sense of identity. He reacted dismissively, and even contemptuously, to my suggestion that identity looms large for some people of mixed race, and that people have struggled long and hard with how to see themselves. "I don't see how it matters," he said.

A day or so later, I described the interview to my father.

"Hmm," Dad said. "Did he look black?"

"He sure did."

"And you said he's only twenty-six?"

"That's right."

"Then one day, his own race is going to sneak up from behind and slap his head."

• • •

There are highly intelligent human beings walking around out there who still say things such as "My grandmother is one-eighth black" or "My best friend is half black." We all bought into this idea for a few hundred years. Whites bought into it because it allowed them to treat millions of people as a subhuman species to be used for their own profit.

But blacks also bought into the one-drop rule. Why? Well, what else were we to do in a continent that ruled blacks were black, no matter how black or white we were?

Some of the ways that black people have bought into this rule are good. Many of us believe in remembering our history, and in sharing a spirit of kinship and attachment with others like us. I am convinced that this community spirit has helped us to survive on this continent, and to keep us from splintering into a gazillion indistinct, divided individuals today.

But at the same time, we have internalized the very worst of North American racist values—light skin is good, and dark skin is bad—and we help perpetuate them to this day.

In my own family, there are ample cases of relatives taking umbrage because their loved ones were choosing darker-skinned blacks.

My grandmother, May Edwards Hill, born in 1896 to a well-to-do, light-skinned family of black Catholics, eloped with my grandfather, Daniel Grafton Hill Jr., also born in 1896, just as my grandfather was preparing to fight for the Allies in the First World War. Indeed, my grandmother told me that what finally sold her on my grandfather was that he came to court her in his United States Army officer's uniform. He swept my grandmother off her feet.

I have to tell you, the uniform didn't sweep my great-grandmother off her feet. This woman's name was Marie Coakley Edwards. There was white blood in her family and, according to my mother, who met her, "She could have passed for white anywhere." Marie was married to a successful dentist, Thomas Edwards, also a light-skinned black man. She lived in a comfortable middle-class house on Linden Street in Washington, D.C., and beat my white maternal grandparents to the punch in purchasing the family's first electric refrigerator. Mostly, I suspect, because she had been taught a certain degree of self-hatred, my great-grandmother Marie Edwards campaigned a holy war against my grandfather.

No matter that he was a good, honest, hard-working, kind, well-educated man. No matter that he was a brilliant storyteller, had a terrific sense of humour, and could knock out piano tunes effortlessly, without training, relying solely on his ear and his long, beautiful, agile ebony fingers. No matter that he had already married my grandmother and not, by the way, for reasons of pregnancy. May didn't have their first child, my aunt Jeanne, until Dan came home from the trenches in France. In my great-grandmother's eyes, my grandfather had a few major strikes against him. He was from a family of modest means. He was from a Methodist family. And worst of all, the man was dark-skinned.

When I look at how this family feud unfolded, I understand better the long-standing, centuries-old, inter-ethnic battles in areas such as the Baltic countries and the Middle East. If my own family members couldn't get along, who in the world am I to judge nations for going to war?

My great-grandmother Edwards offered my grandmother money to leave her husband. I have heard that she offered to send her off to do graduate work at Radcliffe College if only she would leave that dark-skinned black man. Thanks in no small part to this mother-in-law from hell, my grandparents did separate a few times, with four children in the balance, until my grandfather came up with the clever idea of moving May, the children, and himself across the country. It took several days, back then, to travel from Washington, D.C., where Marie Coakley held the fort, to Denver, Colorado, where my grandfather became minister of an African Methodist Episcopal Church. The distance helped to keep

Marie Coakley at bay, and my grandparents never separated again. They loved each other right through a sixty-two-year marriage until Dan died in 1979.

I don't mean to slight the memory of my great-grandmother. She raised four children, and quite capably, I'm sure. She brought into this world my grandmother May, one of the most wonderful people I have ever known, and whose presence I still feel in my life, some fifteen years after her death. And although she had waged the fight of her life to keep my grandmother and grandfather apart, Marie Coakley treated my own father kindly. Indeed, she would slip him a mickey of gin each time he came to visit her in Jersey City when he was on furlough as a soldier in the U.S. Army during the Second World War. I asked my father about this. "She what? This old woman gave you a mickey? Wouldn't she have frowned upon the use of alcohol?"

"No, son, that was your paternal grandmother. *She* was a teetotaller. But Marie Coakley was a Catholic, and the Catholics in our family were never as prudish as the Protestants when it came to knocking back a good stiff drink."

My great-grandmother Edwards wasn't the only racist on the black side of our family. She was simply the most egregious. Her values and actions legitimately represented the values of many, many black people: one does well to "marry light." I'm glad to know about my great-grandmother and the positions she took. It helps me define my own attitudes and identity.

I am acknowledging and staring down this internalized racism, and I will encourage my children to do the same thing. We have inherited a history and a way of thinking, but we are not passive creatures: we will not lie down so that history can march over us. We have the ability—the fortune, the luxury—to say, "You know what? Let's look over this history. I'll take *this* and own it. But I'll take *that* and pitch it out the window."

I'm not one-eighth or one-quarter or one-half black—I'm simply black. And that's because I see blackness as a form of identity, cultural belonging. I'm attached to my heritage. I love the sense of family that comes from giving to and receiving from and living as members of black communities—no matter how disparate they are geographically. *That's* what I'm taking.

Here's what I'm pitching out. We should hate white people. We should hate black people who are darker than we are. We should hate ourselves for not being black enough, or white enough.

What I'm also pitching is the language that has guided and misinformed and indeed blinded our thinking for four centuries. Mulatto? Quadroon? Octoroon? One-quarter black? Half black? All black? Black in this knee but white in the other? These terms I toss out the window, to be buried deep in the snow drifting high outside the farmhouse where I've come to finish this book.

I am black because I say so, because I feel it, know it, and own it. It is not the only thing I am. I am allowed to be a few other things as well. Human is a good starting place. But having seen issues of race and identity raise their heads in North America, I know that when the census form comes around, I'll mark myself down as black.

Acknowledgements

Many people have helped me in my work on *Black Berry, Sweet Juice*, and I want to acknowledge them.

My first thanks go to my parents, Donna and Daniel Hill, and to my sister and brother, Karen and Dan Hill. Their interviews enriched this book substantially, and they read and commented on early drafts. Most important of all, they have each helped to build a supportive family that has always encouraged me to write creatively, and to think empathetically and critically about racial identity.

I thank my children, Andrew, Caroline, and Geneviève Hill, whose unequivocal love always sustains me and who already—despite their tender years—are proud to see me writing and publishing.

Audra Estrones Williams of Halifax, Nova Scotia, was the most resourceful researcher a writer could ever hope to find. Ms. Williams also designed the book cover, created my Web site (www.lawrencehill.com), and offered friendship and encouragement throughout the writing process.

Many people consented to interviews with me, and gave freely of their time and their personal experiences. Not all of their stories made it into the book, but every one of them enriched my understanding of what it means to be of mixed race. The interviewees were Carol Aylward, Adeola Babalola, Nicole Bernhardt, Neil Burgess, Elaine Brooks, Tyson Brown, Debra Capon, Aaron Cavon, Doris Cochran, Stefan Dubowski, Alvin Duncan, Rebeca Dunn-Krahn, Karen Falconer, Jeanne Flateau, Oral Fuentes, Ivan Gibbs, Cheyanne Gorman, Sandra Hardie, Bianca Henwood, Cindy Henwood, Daniel G. Hill, Dan Hill, David Hill, Donna Hill, Karen Hill, Karyn Hood, Kristin Hood, Lorraine Hubbard, Suzette Mayr, Dean Mac-Donald, Deanna MacDonald, Veronica Marsman, Lorraine Mention, Jazz Miller, Jean Moore, Amy Pinto, Lisa Pinto, Catherine Slaney, Laurie Toth, Nicole Virgin, Natalie Wall, Jody Warner, Tracy Williams-Shreve, and two people who will remain anonymous.

Others provided invaluable assistance transcribing the interviews for this book. They include Alexis Brett, Penelope Jackson, Anne Mosher, and Audra Estrones Williams. Michele DuCharme helped with the transcriptions and took the photographs of me for this book and for my Web site.

Dr. Donald Smith, a professor in the history department at the University of Calgary, shared extensive information on the Ku Klux Klan in Oakville, Ontario, explained details about the federal government's *Indian Act*, and has encouraged me for years in writing. Dr. Constance Backhouse, a law professor at the University of Ottawa, and retired archivist Leon Warmski also helped me learn about the Ku Klux Klan in Canada.

Dr. Joseph Cummins, a professor emeritus of genetics at the University of Western Ontario, provided information on issues pertaining to race and genetics; Dr. Minelle Mahtani, a scholar on mixed-race issues and a post-doctoral fellow at the University of British Columbia, read the manuscript and offered thoughtful suggestions to improve it; Dr. Jack Veugelers, an assistant professor of sociology at the University of Toronto, has encouraged my writing for years, and provided many helpful pointers for this book; Dr. James W. St. G. Walker, history professor at the University of Waterloo, provided advice about black history in Canada; and Denys Giguère, Sandra Hardie, Cynthia Martin, and Agnes Van't Bosch commented on early drafts.

I thank Dan Hill, Barry Mann, Matthew McCauley, Kevin Richards, Janet Baker, Beverly Chapin-Hill, and Nikki Harris for their help in arranging for permission to reprint lyrics from the songs "Dark Side of Atlanta" and "McCarthy's Day," which appear on Dan Hill's CDs *Frozen in the Night* and *Longer Fuse*, respectively. Jazz and blues lovers will find Peter Chapman's song "Every Day I Have the Blues," as sung by the one and only Joe Williams, on the CD *Compact Jazz: Count Basie & Joe Williams*.

I want to thank Dean Cooke, my agent, for his support and encouragement.

Special thanks to my editor, Iris Tupholme, who has an uncanny ability to coax the very best effort from me, and who has been gracious, patient, and encouraging throughout the writing of *Black Berry, Sweet Juice*. I also appreciate editorial guidance from Nicole Langlois, Rebecca Vogan, and Janice Weaver on this project.

Finally, I am grateful to the Canada Council for its financial assistance.

Further Reading

I owe a debt to numerous authors, including Carol Camper for her pioneering work as editor of *Miscegenation Blues: Voices of Mixed Race Women* (Sister Vision Press, 1994). Dr. Albert Jacquard, the renowned French geneticist, has written extensively on matters of humanity and race, and his article "Human Rights and Human Nature" in the March 1996 edition of the *UNESCO Courier* helped clarify for me why the concept of race is invalid for human beings.

Other authors and works were of great value to me:

Constance Backhouse, *Colour-Coded: A Legal History of Racism in Canada, 1900–1950* (published for the Osgoode Society for Canadian Legal History by the University of Toronto Press, 1999)

Donald Braman, "Of Race and Immutability" (*UCLA Law Review*, June 1999)

Eldridge Cleaver, *Soul on Ice* (Dell Publishing Co., 1968)

Patricia Hill Collins, *Black Feminist Thought: Knowledge, Consciousness and the Use of the Politics of Empowerment* (Routledge, 2000)

F. James Davis, *Who is Black? One Nation's Definition* (Pennsylvania State University Press, 1993)

Lise Funderburg, *Black, White, Other: Biracial Americans Talk About Race and Identity* (William Morrow, 1994)

Henry Louis Gates Jr., "White Like Me" (*The New Yorker*, June 17, 1996)

Sandra Harding (editor), *"Racial" Economy of Science: Toward a Democratic Future* (Indiana University Press, 1993)

Daniel G. Hill, *Negroes in Toronto: A Sociological Study of a Minority Group* (unpublished doctoral dissertation, University of Toronto, 1960)

James McBride, *The Colour of Water: A Black Man's Tribute to His White Mother* (Riverhead Books, 1996)

Pauli Murray (editor), *States' Laws on Race and Color* (Woman's Division of Christian Service, Methodist Church, 1951)

Jan Nederveen Pieterse, *White on Black: Images of Africa and Blacks in Western Popular Culture* (Yale University Press, 1992)

Sheena Scott and Marie Chen, Counsel for the African Canadian Legal Clinic et al., Factum of the African Canadian Legal Clinic, the Association of Black Social Workers and the Jamaican Canadian Association, Supreme Court of Canada, File #27897, May 22, 2001.

Paul R. Spickard, *Mixed Blood: Intermarriage and Ethnic Identity in Twentieth-Century America* (University of Wisconsin Press, 1989)

Thomas M. Stephens, *Dictionary of Latin American Racial and Ethnic Terminology* (University Press of Florida, 1999)

James W. St. G. Walker, *"Race," Rights and the Law in the Supreme Court of Canada* (Osgoode Society for Canadian Legal History and Wilfrid Laurier University Press, 1997)